Tools for Virtual Teams

Also available from ASQ Quality Press

Team Fitness: A How-To Manual for Building a Winning Work Team
Meg Hartzler and Jane E. Henry, Ph.D.

Mapping Work Processes
Dianne Galloway

Creativity, Innovation, and Quality
Paul E. Plsek

Quality Quotes
Hélio Gomes

Show Me: The Complete Guide to Storyboarding and Problem Solving
Harry I. Forsha

Show Me: Storyboard Workbook and Template
Harry I. Forsha

The Change Agents' Handbook: A Survival Guide for Quality Improvement Champions
David W. Hutton

Understanding and Applying Value-Added Assessment: Eliminating Business Process Waste
William E. Trischler

Avoiding the Pitfalls of Total Quality
Charles C. Poirier and Steven J. Tokarz

LearnerFirst™ Process Management software
with Tennessee Associates International

To request a complimentary catalog of publications, call 800-248-1946.

Tools for Virtual Teams

A Team Fitness Companion

Jane E. Henry, Ph.D.
Meg Hartzler

ASQ Quality Press
Milwaukee, Wisconsin

Tools for Virtual Teams: A Team Fitness Companion
Jane E. Henry, Ph.D., and Meg Hartzler

Library of Congress Cataloging-in-Publication Data
Henry, Jane E., 1934–
    Tools for virtual teams: a team fitness companion / Jane E.
    Henry, Meg Hartzler.
        p.   cm.
    Includes bibliographical references and index.
    ISBN 0-87389-381-6
        1. Teams in the workplace—Handbooks, manuals, etc.   2. Teams in
    the workplace—Computer networks—Handbooks, manuals, etc.
    I. Hartzler, Meg, 1941–   . II. Title.
HD66.H459   1997
658.4'02—dc21   97-14340
                                                                    CIP

10 9 8 7 6 5 4 3 2 1

ISBN 0-87389-381-6

Acquisitions Editor: Roger Holloway
Project Editor: Kelley Cardinal

ASQ Mission: To facilitate continuous improvement and increase customer satisfaction by identifying, communicating, and promoting the use of quality principles, concepts, and technologies; and
thereby be recognized throughout the world as the leading authority on, and champion for, quality.

Attention: Schools and Corporations
ASQ Quality Press books, videotapes, audiotapes, and software are available at quantity discounts
with bulk purchases for business, educational, or instructional use. For information, please
contact ASQ Quality Press at 800-248-1946, or write to ASQ Quality Press, P.O. Box 3005,
Milwaukee, WI 53201-3005.

For a free copy of the ASQ Quality Press Publications Catalog, including ASQ membership
information, call 800-248-1946.

Printed in the United States of America

♾ Printed on acid-free paper

American Society for Quality

Quality Press
611 East Wisconsin Avenue
Milwaukee, Wisconsin 53202

Our Vision

Our vision for this book-writing project was to use our best thinking and experiences to put together a manual that is readable, practical, personal, straightforward, and takes the mystery out of how to build an effective team.

Our vision for its use is that this text will become dog-eared, coffee-stained, and yellow-highlighted, with its corners folded down, and falling open naturally to certain pages.

Meg and Jane

Contents

Foreword

Jane and Meg have done it again. These two leaders in team effectiveness and team building have come together to create a resource useful for organizations challenged by the ever-increasing competitive demands of our global marketplace. The authors have taken what they have learned from the experience with their first book, Team Fitness, *to focus on a new dimension of team building that rarely gets attention but is growing in popularity. The "virtual team" is not only diverse in terms of culture, gender, age, and nationality, but it is also composed of members who are geographically dispersed. In reviewing the literature, there is little written about virtual teams—those teams that must be highly productive within short time frames when members are positioned across nations or continents and in remote locations around the world.*

Building a virtual team is an exciting challenge for line managers. They must draw on a particular set of tools and techniques to create dispersed teams rapidly and sustain their productivity over extended time periods. As we move to the twenty-first century, this capability will increase in demand. Meg and Jane have "cracked the code" in helping managers achieve operational and financial goals with dispersed teams. The authors have provided exercises and team building processes that address this unique condition and build a foundation for further growth in this area.

In reviewing this book, I was again impressed by the authors' commitment to extend their knowledge and experience by graciously offering their team building technology to the world in a user-friendly way. While most experts jealously guard their technology, Jane and Meg have shared what they have learned as a way of generating more powerful processes and subsequent effectiveness to teams and leaders who have the desire, but need the particular how-to.

The way to benefit from this resource is to use it systematically, step-by-step, one piece at a time, to build and maintain highly productive and effective dispersed work teams. Today's teams come together to use their diverse ideas and capabilities to generate business results and competitive advantage. The more tools they have to meet that challenge, the better they will perform now and into the twenty-first century.

Good reading!!

> Stephen K. Merman, Ed.D.
> Past President
> The American Society for Training and Development

Preface

Just when you thought you were getting used to working in teams—
just when you could start to see the real advantages of having
people with varied experience, perspectives, and approaches working on one team challenge—just when you learned some of the key
factors that make your teams really work, or even just survive—it
got harder!

- What if your teams were made up of members who were not
  located in the same place? What if they rarely met together in
  person?

- What if they had never known or seen each other before
  becoming members of the team?

- What if some of them spoke different languages and were in
  different time zones?

- *What if they didn't even work for your company and had no allegiance to the organization you represent?*

- *What if the only thing they really shared was a common database that each could access on the Internet?*

- *What if they would probably never work together again after this project?*

Now we know what that first person meant who said, "Nobody ever told us it would be easy!"

We wrote our first book, Team Fitness: A How-To Manual for Building a Winning Work Team, *to help team members and leaders deal with and capitalize on the many opportunities of teaming. While working with countless teams to implement those ideas, we have found more and more examples of geographically dispersed teams that need to function as well as if they were located in one particular place. We ourselves have been members of such teams and have experienced the complex and challenging conditions under which many of them work. We have seen teams that sputtered and died—too splintered and unfocused to get real results. We have also seen teams that thrived, taking on energy as the heat was turned up. We wrote this book for those teams that wish to stay connected and keep the spirit of teaming, even when they work mostly on their own as individuals.*

Effective team leaders know that team fitness is a journey—a disciplined focus of working to improve excellence. With Tools for Virtual Teams: A Team Fitness Companion, teams and leaders *will find enhancements for their fitness approach. Once they have laid out their fitness plan,* Tools for Virtual Teams provides the right emphasis needed for geographically dispersed teams. They will receive guidance on how to target their exercises to the challenges that dispersed teams commonly face.*

Used alone, Tools for Virtual Teams gets those teams off to the right start. They may then choose to look to Team Fitness to add to their long-term, sustained approach.

In any case, the teams that focus on building effectiveness through using these exercises will gain the competence and confidence needed to perform at their best. Our vision remains constant. Our challenge continues to grow. Best wishes to you and your virtual team!

ACKNOWLEDGMENTS

We wish to acknowledge the help of the many people who provided support and information. Special thanks go to the people who allowed us to interview them about their work with virtual teams. These leaders gave us invaluable information and advice. They are: John Coleman, CEO, ViA Marketing and Design of Portland, Maine, Columbus, Ohio, and Zurich, Switzerland; Richard A. Gould, Supplier Engineering, Western Digital Corporation of Irvine, California; Judy Issokson, Program Manager, Management Development, Sun Microsystems of Mountain View, California;

---

*See the Fitness Meter in *Team Fitness* (Hartzler and Henry 1994).

Susan McPherson, President/CEO, Creative Communications Consultants, Inc. of Minneapolis, Minnesota; and Colonel Alan B. Thomas, Commander, 67th Intelligence Wing, U.S. Air Force in San Antonio, Texas.

Special thanks go to our illustrator, Peter Hesse, and Kelley Cardinal, our helpful and understanding editor with ASQ Quality Press. Jane's husband, Jack Snider, a master of the King's English and ace jargon-detector, gave us long editing hours and support.

More special thanks to Tea L. Del Alma Silvestre of Destra, whose phone calling, editing, and formatting saved many hours, and to Ruth Eastman of Destra for helping us keep the door to the rest of the world closed while we wrote. Thanks to Pamela Dennis, David Hannegan, and Al Starkey of Destra for many activities they've done with our clients and for constant encouragement.

And of course, thanks to the teams we work with that are our teachers every day!

Meg and Jane

Introduction

Welcome to the age of the networked organization. You and millions of team leaders and members may belong to geographically dispersed—that is, virtual—teams. Somehow you will need to accomplish projects and assignments without the advantages of being located centrally, able to meet face-to-face. You are entering uncharted territory. There are few road maps to help you succeed. Ultimately, you will need to operate differently in order to find the same kind of creativity and synergy that often comes from working together as an intact team.

You are entering uncharted territory.

Although dispersed teams are not necessarily a new phenomenon, they are becoming more prevalent—and their numbers will continue to expand in the future. It is estimated that 8.4 million

U.S. workers are currently working in dispersed teams and that by 1998, that number will exceed 13 million (Townsend, DeMarie, and Hendrickson 1996.) If you aren't working this way now, chances are that you will be—soon!

WHAT ARE THE DRIVERS OF VIRTUAL TEAMS?

1. With increasing globalization in the market-place, organizations must bring their members closer to the customer to be responsive to the customer's needs. Some actually share office space with their customers.

> We are tenants on Air Force bases. Our team members are living with the customers we are there to assist. I tell them to pretend they are sponges, soaking up ideas and adapting them for our work. This increases our new ideas by 200 percent. We wouldn't get that if our whole group was located together.
>
> **Colonel Alan B. Thomas**
> **Commander**
> **67th Intelligence Wing,**
> **U.S. Air Force**

2. As competition grows more fierce and the amount of expertise and information expands exponentially, there is a need to bring diverse talents and expertise to bear on complex projects and to customize solutions to meet the demands of the market.

> **O**ur virtual teams include an art director, a copy writer, and a media and production person. The account manager is a full-time employee, team leader, and liaison with the client. We have been working this way for 18 years. I'm glad there's finally a name for it so our clients can understand it better.
>
> **Susan McPherson**
> **President/CEO**
> **Creative Communications Consultants, Inc.**

3. Dispersed teams can leverage the expertise of the organization by putting people together on a project without relocating them. Companies can pull in outside resources for a project without adding people to the payroll. Small companies can assemble teams of diverse talents from anywhere in the world.

> **W**e can find world-class people to work with big clients. We can marshal the resources of a much larger organization.
>
> **John Coleman**
> **President**
> **ViA Marketing & Design, Inc.**

4. Advances in technology—teleconferencing, the Internet, video-conferencing, and computers have made virtual teaming possible. Corporations, large and small, are putting these technologies to work with some surprising results. Shy people often thrive in this environment. Writing may be easier for them than speaking, especially when they are comfortable sharing information and working with computers.

> **D**ispersed teams are great equalizers. People with disabilities can contribute remotely; people with English as a second language often communicate effectively with these alternative methods. Dealing with different time zones is less of an obstacle.
>
> **Judy Issokson**
> **Program Manager, Management Development**
> **Sun Microsystems**

Virtual teams are a reality. They are not inherently better or worse than conventional teams. Like other teams, they face challenges and barriers as they go about their business. This book offers specific tools and techniques that will enhance effectiveness in the areas these teams find particularly challenging.

Who are these teams? When we talk about dispersed, virtual, or networked teams we are not referring to those opportunistic networks that come together quickly to create a joint venture. Our focus, and the focus of this book, is today's growing organizational model that uses technology to link—in a dramatic way—the people, assets, and ideas from many parts of the world that are needed for today's complex business challenges.

These virtual teams are groups of people who work closely together even though they are geographically separated by miles or even continents. They may be intact workgroups that work together indefinitely, or they may be cross-functional groups brought together to tackle a project for a finite period of time. Their primary interaction over time is through a combination of technologies such as the telephone, overnight mail, fax, a shared database, the Internet, email, PC-to-PC hook-ups, shared computer screens, and/or video-conferencing.

The concepts described in this book will need to be adapted to the technology available to the team. With technologies changing at an exponential rate, any recommendation of a particular medium would limit this book's usefulness. Having said that, use whatever means you have to keep in touch with each other, keep the momentum going, and do whatever it takes to get the job done.

We work from the following characteristics to clarify which teams are virtual or dispersed.

- Members are mutually accountable for team results—not just coordinating separate accountabilities.

- Members are dispersed geographically (nationally or internationally).

- The team works apart more than in the same location.

> Ours is a networked organization. Corporate headquarters and product development are located in the States. Our manufacturing is in Singapore and Malaysia, and our suppliers can be found all over the globe. We work in virtual teams on a daily basis.
>
> **Richard A. Gould**
> **Supplier Engineering**
> **Western Digital Corporation**

- The team solves problems and makes decisions jointly.

- The team usually consists of no more than 20 members.

Used effectively, teams that work together in this way can realize significant benefits or payoffs. For instance, teams can be built with members who might not otherwise be available because of a lack of proximity. This means the best people can be potential team members, regardless of location, and membership can easily include outsiders such as consultants. Membership can also remain fluid and change easily, because there is no relocation lag time or cost.

> **M**embers can have flexibility, balance of work and home life. They say, "You don't have to fix the rest of your life around your work." They feel that they really make a contribution and are trusted. The work is autonomous and provides more variety and professional growth.
>
> **Judy Issokson**
> **Program Manager, Management Development**
> **Sun Microsystems**

Beverly Geber (1995) proposes some positive possibilities that can come from using a shared database, which can then become a major organizer for the team. Because information is easily available and accessible by any team member when it is housed on a common database, newcomers are quickly brought up to speed and all members can stay current independently. The somewhat anonymous nature of participation has the potential to minimize some of the political barriers arising from fear of repercussion or domination of the group's process.

For these potentials to be achieved, significant challenges and barriers must be addressed. For instance, in virtual teams, language, culture, and style differences may be accentuated because of the losses in communication when body language, subtle tones, and facial gestures are not available to add to the spoken word. Misinterpretations and misunderstandings may be heightened if there is no direct way to work through what one member may think she heard in a phone

> **W**hen people don't "live" together, they cooperate more. They don't have to fight for their ideas. You listen to what is being said, and look at the ideas rather than the person.
>
> **Susan McPherson**
> **President/CEO**
> **Creative Communications Consultants, Inc.**

conference meeting. Individual interpretations may create situations where each team member unknowingly "does his own thing" rather than promoting the team's agenda. The lack or void of relationship and trust may bring about the tendency to work to one's own advantage, causing problems for other team members. In addition, isolation, loneliness, and the feeling of disconnectedness can erode energy and lessen commitment to the team. These challenges will be explored in more depth in the three tools and techniques sections of this book.

Take heart! Some experience is in place to help guide those who find themselves leading or participating in a virtual team. Incorporating the following critical considerations can help ensure a high probability of success.

Up front—when the team is formed

- Spend time and money to bring the team together in the forming stage for a face-to-face start-up session. This helps team members know one another, learn idiosyncrasies and quirks, form friendships, and create systems by learning common methodologies and a shared language to use in their work together. It also allows some relationship and trust to form before moving to electronic and voice communication.

- Even if you can't get together face-to-face, develop and understand a clear direction and plan for what the team intends to do, and values for how to accomplish its goals. Make sure these are shared by all members. This creates the "same sheet of music" for the team and allows for individual decision making and action to move the team forward appropriately.

- Train members in the methodologies and software necessary for working together, such as problem solving, database management, and project planning.

The most important part of the project is the up-front time. This is when personalities gel, friendships are formed, and members get used to one another's work styles and temperaments. It's also the time for finding out, for instance, that when Kurt says no, he's adamant about it and doesn't tolerate jawboning. Trying to fathom personality quirks like that via computer is much more difficult and time-consuming, and can damage the rapport of the team if tensions develop into flame wars via email.

John Spencer
Worldwide manager for design and development of single-use cameras
Eastman Kodak Co.
(Geber 1995, 38)

- Put in place formal operating agreements developed by all team members for what they commit to do or not to do. These cover things all the way from what topics are discussed, to how often everyone will update the database, to how breaking agreements will be handled or how conflicts will be managed.

Once the team is underway

- Management and communication are formal processes with specific and direct responsibilities laid out and little left to chance. Sharing of critical information is a top priority, and anything that slows the progress of information must be corrected immediately.

- Expect and require competent performance. Incompetence or lack of accountability can't be tolerated.

- Don't put aside the human side of the arrangement. Ways to have personal contact and informal social time need to be built in periodically. Make special efforts to create fun, celebrate progress and successes, and show personality.

> **T**rust comes from performance. It's trust that springs from competence. If I see this person is going to do a first-rate job with the information I provide, that he won't undercut it, won't embarrass me, then I'm more likely to trust him.
>
> **Lee Sproull**
> **Professor of Management**
> **Boston University**
> (Geber 1995, 39)

SUMMARY

Remember that building fitness is an iterative, ongoing job. Dispersed teams, like all others, must follow through on the good things they put in place up front. Regular milestone checks and project planning reviews are critical. The habit of discussing team progress, both on project results and on effective teaming, is required in order to keep in place—and build on—a solid start. Teams must regularly assess how things are going, pick exercises and activities that fit their current needs, carry out those activities, and execute the agreements and plans made. A checklist for this purpose can be found in appendix A. Periodically, celebrate programs and milestones. That's what makes any fitness program work!

The Team Fitness Model and Virtual Teams

T eam leaders and managers who find themselves in the position of building a new team or revitalizing an existing team can benefit from having models, tools, and guidelines to shape their work.

In our previous book, *Team Fitness: A How-To Manual for Building a Winning Work Team* (Hartzler and Henry 1994), we developed a model for teams to follow to become more effective. In this section we will briefly describe this model and suggest what areas need more emphasis as teams work in dispersed locations.

To navigate through complex situations, conflicting demands, and limited resources, teams need fitness training and the tools to get things done. The four areas of team exercises and activities that help the team get fit are

- Customer focus

- Direction

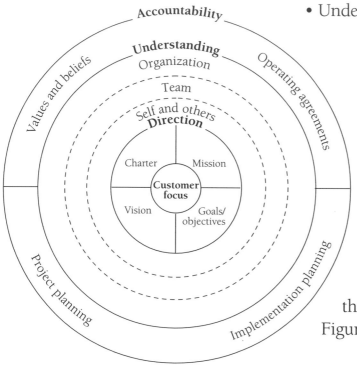

Figure 1. Team fitness.

- Understanding

- Accountability

Just as everyone knows it takes focus and commitment to maintain fitness through exercise, diet, and good habits, the team must dedicate time and energy to strengthen itself in each of these four areas.

The Team Fitness Model shows the relationship of the key areas (see Figure 1).

FITNESS AREA 1: CUSTOMER FOCUS

Definition. Customer focus is about getting clear on the needs, expectations, and priorities of those who receive your work and ensuring that those expectations shape the requirements for the products and services your team provides.

Factors. Customer focus has two parts: *identification of customers* and *clarification of customers' expectations.*

What's Different for Virtual Teams? Many virtual teams have been established to work with specific client groups. These teams often have a liaison person or coordinator who spends a good deal of time with the client, sometimes actually officing on the client's premises. Each team member may reside at a different client site. Other teams do not have this advantage— often none of them are located close to the client. The difference is that team members are not located together, so they cannot all be close to the client.

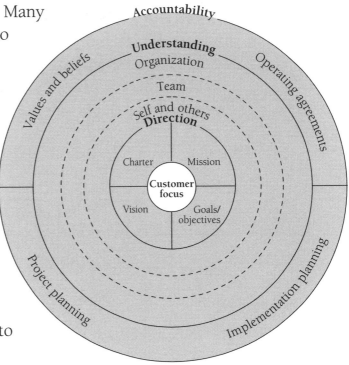

Figure 2. The first fitness area—customer focus.

The Good News. When members are close to the client, the team has a direct link for clarity about customer expectations.

The Challenge. If one person offices with the customer, other team members may rarely or never see the customer. The team may have to develop a "line of sight" to their sponsor to find out more about customer needs. Pulling together an understanding of client needs and priorities, when dispersed, is difficult and demands the utmost clarity of communication. The trick is to get an in-depth level of understanding that is shared among all team members.

FITNESS AREA 2: DIRECTION

Definition. Direction defines the unique contribution of the team, from its broadest purposes to its specific actions and activities. Direction shows the fit of the team's and the organization's purpose.

Factors. Direction is composed of the following four factors.

1. *Charter*—Clear understandings between the team and its sponsor

2. *Vision*—A shared mental image of what the team wants to contribute in the future; an ideal state

3. *Mission*—The purpose and unique contribution of the team that will make the vision come true

4. *Goals and objectives*—Broad statements of the desired end results with objectives that spell out the specific actions and activities needed to obtain those results

What's Different for Virtual Teams? Gaining commitment and alignment around the team's purpose is best done in a face-to-face meeting where the team builds its own vision, where the members work together to determine its mission, and where the chartering sponsor can work directly with team members. Goals and objectives are a natural outcome of this process. When teams are in remote locations, this alignment and commitment are more difficult to generate. Virtual teams must find a way to get this done up front, in the early stages of working together.

The Good News. Most sponsors recognize that teams need a special effort to come together, particularly at the beginning of the project. This will allow team members to become clear and to align themselves with the project. The awareness of the need to come together for this purpose may already exist, or it may need to be built.

The Challenge. Dispersed teams may need to fight for enough up-front face-to-face time to give everyone a true common understanding. It is easy to be "almost on the same wavelength" but not really aligned.

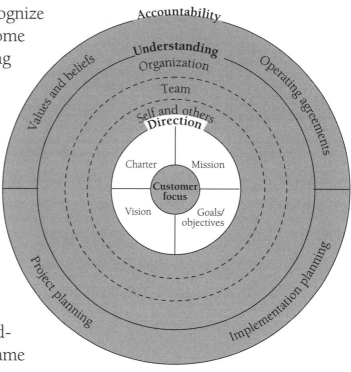

Figure 3. The second fitness area—direction.

FITNESS AREA 3: UNDERSTANDING

Definition: Understanding means learning and interpreting the inherent nature of ourselves, our team members, and our organization as well as the impact of that nature on the work at hand.

Factors: There are three factors in this fitness area.

1. *Self and others*—Increasing awareness of and using the strengths and differences in each team member, including yourself

2. *Teams*—Understanding the dynamics that occur in teamwork approaches to problem solving and decision making

3. *Organization*—Understanding the norms and culture of the organization and how to get things done in that culture

What's Different for Virtual Teams? Virtual teammates do not have face-to-face interaction on a daily basis. They have less knowledge and understanding of each other as people. Because some members are at different locations or even outsiders to the organization, there may be little or varying understanding of the organization's direction, values, and goals.

The Good News. A tremendous diversity and richness of potential team members is opened up. Not only can they come from different geographic areas but also from different industries, cultures, working styles, and backgrounds of experience.

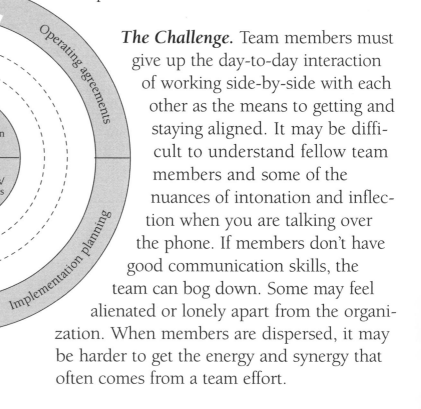

The Challenge. Team members must give up the day-to-day interaction of working side-by-side with each other as the means to getting and staying aligned. It may be difficult to understand fellow team members and some of the nuances of intonation and inflection when you are talking over the phone. If members don't have good communication skills, the team can bog down. Some may feel alienated or lonely apart from the organization. When members are dispersed, it may be harder to get the energy and synergy that often comes from a team effort.

Figure 4. The third fitness area—understanding.

FITNESS AREA 4: ACCOUNTABILITY

Definition. Accountability is the process of mutually agreeing on what results the team is expected to achieve with specific plans and activities, and a sense for how the team will be responsible to the organization and to one another.

Factors. There are four factors that influence the team's accountability.

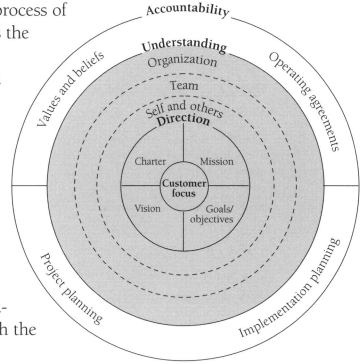

Figure 5. The fourth fitness area—accountability.

1. *Values and beliefs*—The beliefs held by the organization and the team, by which the team is expected to live

2. *Operating agreements*—The ways team members agree to behave and work together

3. *Project planning*—The planning methods used to ensure that the right things are done, done right, done in the right sequence, and done on schedule

4. *Implementation planning*—The planning methods used to ensure that the project plans and the work of the team will be accepted by the rest of the organization

What's Different for Virtual Teams? Dispersed teammates cannot infer values and beliefs from the behaviors of others, because they are not observing their teammates in daily work. Nor can they run down the hall for quick "check-ins" or have hallway conversations to move things along informally.

The Good News. Virtual teams can build a credo of how they will work together that makes many choices clear before decisions are made. Most organizations that work effectively in this manner have a set of principles or values that each member agrees to follow. These then, rather than policies and procedures, guide the daily decisions members make on behalf of the team. This can be done as part of the face-to-face start-up work the team does together, and it will serve as a way to prevent things that could otherwise go awry. Also, teammates can receive common training on the information technology they will use as well as methodologies such as problem solving or decision making. This training creates a common language and approach that is critical to dispersed teams' success.

The Challenge. Ensuring that the team has a set of values or operating agreements that everyone can understand and agree on can be difficult and time-consuming work. It can also be tough to understand the implications of values at the behavioral level. Many organizations are also prone to shortchange the team on the amount of training given to ensure that a shared methodology is in place.

The Rest of the Story. In the book *Team Fitness* we used research, theory, and our own years of experience with teams to provide simple, pragmatic techniques and activities to raise productivity, profitability, and commitment through teamwork in the four key areas. Our goals remains to help teams become "fit"—able to handle the challenges and complex situations they face in a way that not only brings superior results, but also builds their competence and confidence as a team.

The Team Fitness Model will be particularly useful to dispersed teams in the initial start-up phase as they come together to define, clarify, and get ready to work together from afar. Some activities from the book *Team Fitness* that are especially appropriate for dispersed teams are listed below.

Customer Focus	Direction	Understanding	Accountability
• Who Is the Customer?	• Project or Task Team New Team Charter	• In-Depth Intros	• Values Statements
• What Do Our Customers Want and Expect From Us?	• A One-Day Visioning Meeting	• What Makes Us Tick?	• If—Then—Then
	• Mission Statement	• Are We a Team or a Work Group?	• Operating Agreements
	• Goals and Objectives—Top Down		• Negotiating Ground Rules
	• Which Goals Have Priority?		• Team Responsibility Chart
			• ABC Priorities
			• Implementation Responsibility Chart
			• Stakeholder Support
			• Critical Success Factors

This book, *Tools for Virtual Teams,* is also meant to be a how-to manual with specific emphasis on achieving the same high level of teamwork when a team is dispersed. We have provided a menu of activities from which to select. You will need to assess your own situation and your own team, then pick the techniques that work best for you. The choices and sequence will vary according to the time your team will be together and your starting point in terms of trust, success, and relationship. Over time, your team can take a step-by-step approach to diagnosing your team's needs, planning for team activities, and carrying out those activities. Dispersed teams need to develop fitness just like any other teams. The habit of continuously improving teamwork is critical to long-term success. Special focus on the challenges of geographic dispersion will help significantly to strengthen the approach.

This book is designed to help leaders deal with the following specific challenges that are magnified by the distance between team members. Each section that follows focuses on one of the challenges, giving the reader tips and exercises to make the virtual team more effective.

Challenge 1: Direction/Focus. Setting a clear path and purpose that specifies focus and defines the outcomes of the team's work with clear accountabilities for members. This challenge is similar to what all teams face when working on direction and accountability in the Team Fitness Model.

Challenge 2: Values/Principles, Operating Agreements. Establishing the values and agreements that clarify expectations, methodologies that are to be followed, and desired culture of the team. This challenge is about accountability—in particular, being accountable to the higher order of team values and to the needs of the customer. It is also about being counted on to use the methods that are easy for other members to understand and accept.

Challenge 3: Synergy/Communication. Creating an elaborate formal and informal communication approach that replaces face-to-face interaction; finding the spark of energy and excitement that bonds team members and creates conditions for risk-taking and commitment. Challenge 3 is a *Team Fitness* understanding issue where the team's actions either take away from or enhance the internal ability of team members to work with each other (Hartzler and Henry 1994).

Challenge 1:
Direction/Focus

A clear definition of the desired outcome of the team's work is critical. All teams need to have a vision, a mission, and goals and objectives with individual accountability to the

Command and control is harder to "manage." My field commanders are pretty autonomous. I probably know 3 percent to 5 percent of what they do on a daily basis; however, that percent is very important to me and they know it. My commanders need to know what I want and I have to be clear about what is and is not negotiable.

I tell them, "This is like a three-lane highway. We're all going to the same place, going in the same direction. We've agreed on the destination. You can drive in any lane you want. If you choose the right lane, you cannot go so slowly as to impede others. If you choose the left lane, don't drive so recklessly as to endanger the rest of us."

Colonel Alan B. Thomas
Commander
67th Intelligence Wing, U.S. Air Force

team's work. When teams are dispersed, it is easier to lose sight of the goal, the path forward, and the ultimate desired results. Virtual teams are in more danger of going off course with no one to notice and make midcourse corrections.

DIRECTION BEGINS WITH THE FORMATION OF THE TEAM

When the virtual team meets for the first time (at the kick-off), the leader, coordinator, or sponsor must be very clear about the focus of work and the end result. All the background of understanding and the business case for the work of the team needs to be supplied,

When teams are dispersed, it's easier to lose sight of the goal.

as well as any specific decisions that have already been made about the team's direction. Successful teams then usually create a vision and a mission for themselves, making sure these are aligned with the need.

THE CLIENT OFTEN SETS THE FOCUS OR DIRECTION

Many teams meet with the client to get a clear perspective of their needs and wants. One person may be designated to work directly with the client, coordinating efforts for the rest of the team. Virtual teams have been described as being more objective in customer relations because they do not see the client so often. If, however, the team shares office space with the client, the advantage is that team members are in constant touch with the needs of the customer and the language and approach that are most useful for the customer's environment.

THE TEAM SPONSOR HAS A MAJOR ROLE TO PLAY IN THE FORMATION OF A NEW TEAM

It is the responsibility of the sponsor to ensure that the team can see the connection between its own efforts and the strategic goals of the organization. If there is no common organizational or national culture, such as when team members are from different countries or from outside the organization, then there is no way that team members can guess the link between their work and the corporate strategy. If this is your situation, building a "line of sight" connection to the sponsor from the team is critical to keeping the correct focus.

UP-FRONT WORK IS IMPERATIVE FOR A TEAM TO SUCCEED

Starting with a face-to-face meeting at the kick-off of a new team project is a necessary investment. Teams form more slowly if they don't have the opportunity to meet in person. Some groups that meet only electronically never gel—never really get off the ground. This meeting provides the necessary clarity of focus and direction, and gives people a chance to establish relationships and feel a part of the team.

An example plan for a typical one-day start-up meeting can be found in appendix B.

> We bring the team together at the beginning of a really big campaign. It's more efficient. Then later we communicate by phone, fax, overnight mail, computer, whatever it takes to get the job done. Working with virtual teams requires me to be more organized and clear on direction. I can't walk into their offices and check on things. I have to be careful to write everything down and then build in a checking mechanism.
>
> **Susan McPherson**
> **President/CEO**
> **Creative Communications Consultants, Inc.**

When teams come together for their start-up session, they must get clarity on things from the broadest big-picture perspective down to their individual responsibilities. A funnel diagram helps show how teams often define direction.

The Funnel—Clarifying Team Direction

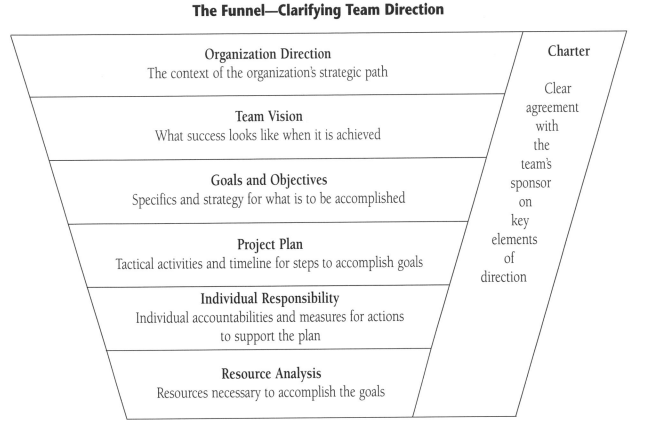

Organization Direction
The context of the organization's strategic path

Team Vision
What success looks like when it is achieved

Goals and Objectives
Specifics and strategy for what is to be accomplished

Project Plan
Tactical activities and timeline for steps to accomplish goals

Individual Responsibility
Individual accountabilities and measures for actions
to support the plan

Resource Analysis
Resources necessary to accomplish the goals

Charter

Clear agreement with the team's sponsor on key elements of direction

Source: Adapted from GE Plastics Commercial Education & Development

SUMMARY

One of the basic challenges to virtual teams is the danger of losing focus—losing sight of the purpose and specific mission of the work. A big part of the solution is investing the time to achieve a real and shared sense of clarity in the beginning.

DIRECTION EXERCISE 1
Start at the End

Workout Plan

When to use
When you want to help team members make real or concrete the image of the future state they are trying to create. By projecting ahead as if it already exists, the team can get a clear idea of the goal. This is very useful for broad and ambiguous projects involving significant change, and helps create the context for making realistic plans. Team members need to have done some project start-up work in advance so that they understand the nature of the work and what they are being asked to accomplish.

Materials
Current project planning documents to use as references

Time
One to two hours, plus some advanced preparation time if remote

Purpose/objectives
- To ensure alignment and consistency in each team member's understanding of the vision

- To help team members envision what the new state will look like in concrete behavioral terms

Warm-up

Ask team members to look ahead and imagine a time when the project is successfully implemented—the time when the vision has become a reality. Imagine that you are videotaping the new situation. What has happened because of the work of the team? What do you see, hear, and feel as you watch people perform their daily tasks and activities?

If face-to-face, such as in a team start-up meeting, do all of the steps at one time. If remote, do aerobics steps 1 and 2 via phone conferences and then complete step 3 as part of a whole team meeting (phone or video conference). If sharing a database, the input from step 2 can be entered into the database and all members can review it before their next conference meeting.

Aerobics

1. Ask people to work in pairs and describe to each other what they saw. Capture two to four sentences that describe what they saw.

2. Ask two pairs to work together and again describe what they saw. Build a new two- to four-sentence description that represents the thinking of all four team members.

3. Come together as a team and build a statement by consensus that represents the image of the change.

Cooldown

When people "see" activities and tasks in the new way, some will be excited and energized. Others will uncover images that make them feel uncomfortable. Be sure to spend enough time talking about the images so that individuals have been understood and have connected their own personal energy and vision to the work of the team. This is what promotes true commitment and creates conditions for risk taking. Make sure that whatever they build is saved so you can come back to it in the future to see what has been realized.

Note: Some groups may prefer to build a visual picture of themselves in the future as the end product of this activity.

DIRECTION EXERCISE 2
Purpose Statement

Workout Plan

When to use
When you are forming the team and want members to gain understanding of their work at a deeper level.

Time
One to two hours

Materials
Flip charts and markers

Purpose/objectives

- To rise above the immediate deliverables of the project and consider the underlying higher purpose of the work that relates to the organization's strategy and future and to each individual's vision or purpose

- To show the link to how the team's work will address a desired element of the organization's future

Warm-up
Ask team members to think silently of the "wish" they have for how their work would make a difference and how it would connect to a personal vision or value each individual team member holds.

Aerobics

Collaboratively write the purpose statement in three sections.

1. Our purpose is to . . . (shows the work itself—mission)

2. In a way that . . . (shows how you will work—values)

3. So that . . . (shows the underlying results/payoff—strategic intent)

Example

> *Our purpose is to* create a fair and equitable compensation system *in a way that* builds stakeholder commitment and support and rewards what we truly believe and need *so that* the system will motivate all individuals to accomplish the organization's objectives, thereby ensuring long-term profitability and value for us as a firm.

Cooldown

When individuals have written their statements, ask them to share and give the thinking that underlies their statement. When all statements are read, look for common themes and build one statement that represents the group consensus (optional).

DIRECTION EXERCISE 3
Problem Statement

Workout Plan

When to use
Teams are often formed to solve problems. When your team's focus is to problem solve, a clear statement of the problem can act like the mission statement does for another kind of team.

Time
Thirty minutes to one hour

Purpose/objectives
- To build a clear, shared descriptive statement of the problem so that team members are sure of and in agreement about the nature of their work

Materials
Flip chart and markers

Warm-up
If meeting face-to-face, ask each member to relate an anecdote or share a perception or event that has to do with the problem the team has been asked to resolve. The purpose of this part of the exercise is to hear different perceptions or aspects of the problem. If the meeting is remote, create a place on the database or fax around a sheet where each member fills in the blanks as shown in the example.

Example

My Perception of the Problem	The Impact This Has in the Organization
• In their evaluations, our people are rewarded for their contributions as individuals, not for teamwork	• Teamwork is given lip service but many people still "look out for number one," and "Lone Ranger" acts are very common, eroding our effectiveness as teams.
•	•

Aerobics

1. Thinking back to the perceptions shared, write collaboratively the statement of the problem in three sections.

   • The nature of the problem (*what*—describe the specific thing that is occurring)

   • The impact of the problem (*why it matters*—summarize the impact on the organization)

   • The time frame of the problem (*how long*—how much time has passed while this has occurred?)

2. Optional—Small groups could draft statements and then bring them together to build one statement for the team.

Example

> "Turnover has increased from 5 percent (annualized) to 10 percent (annualized) over the last six months, increasing our employee acquisition costs by 35 percent."

Cooldown

End the session by going around one at a time (round-robin), asking each individual to state one implication based on the problem statement that will affect the work of the team.

DIRECTION EXERCISE 4
Creating a Process Map

Workout Plan

When to use
Use this when the team is determining the scope of the project and coming to agreement on what it is really trying to accomplish. Doing project work is a process that can be analyzed just like any other process.

Time
Two to three hours

Materials
If face-to-face, you will need several packages of index cards (white and colored), masking tape, and markers. If remote, some total quality or continuous improvement software packages have process mapping features. This could be used, with members brainstorming and adding to the common database version before a specified date. Meeting time is then used to discuss and finalize the map based on the previous individual drafts.

Purpose/objectives
- To develop a shared working picture of the project process

- To determine boundaries and the scope of the work so that it has a clear beginning and end

- To understand the influence of inputs into the project work and of stakeholder expectations of results

Warm-up
Name the process of the project, starting with a verb (ends in *-ing*)—for example, "developing a succession planning system" or "rewriting the partner compensation plan."

Aerobics
1. Determine the output of the project—for example, "system for succession planning implemented."

2. List customers and other key stakeholders of your work.

3. You can list their expectations now (beside each customer), or this part can be done at another time.

4. List the inputs that are necessary to this project.

5. Briefly list the suppliers of those inputs.

6. Bound the project. Determine the project scope by deciding what the start and stop points are for the project. This determines how "macro" a process is—a large encompassing system—or whether the project is aimed at something more micro—for example, a subprocess of the larger process.

Example

Process Map

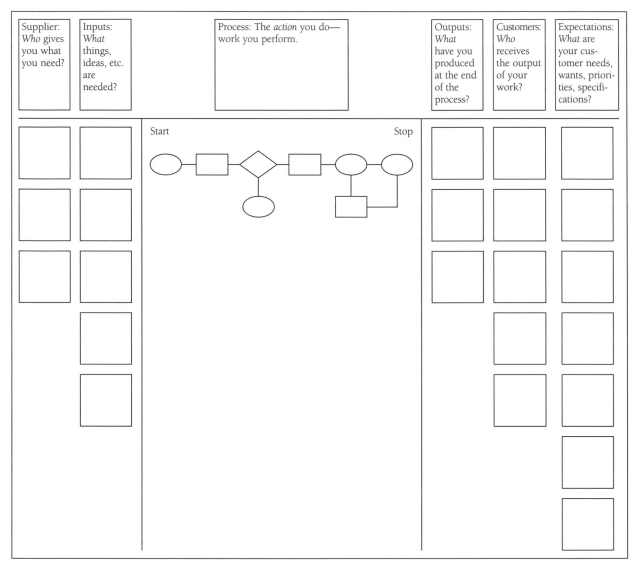

Cooldown

This analysis can be very thorough as you move through each of the headers. Early in the project, such as during team start-up, you may want to move quickly through aerobics steps 2 through 5 and focus mainly on determining the start and stop points to help define the scope of the project. Then come back to do the rest of the analysis in more depth at a later time.

DIRECTION EXERCISE 5
High-Involvement Planning

Workout Plan

When to use

- In project start-up to develop roles for the core team and expanded stakeholders for the project

- Throughout the project to plan for participation and necessary input in key team meetings and decision points; as part of input and data gathering activities, events, and communications about project progress

- When you must determine who needs to be "sold" and at what point in the project, and how to emphasize involvement vs. "selling"

Time
Varies

Materials
See Direction Exercise 7: Force Field Analysis
Also see Direction Exercise 6: Resource Analysis

This activity is most appropriate for a face-to-face meeting. Updates can be done in remote meetings as needed.

Purpose/objectives

- To ensure that the project team plans tasks and activities as a *core team* and also with the involvement of a broader group of stakeholders as an *expanded team.*

- To expand the influence of the core team and promote commitment and buy-in by involving key stakeholders in team activities periodically throughout the life of the project rather than selling them on the end product that the team developed.

Warm-up

Write the specific project description and desired outcomes to focus thinking for the planning process, or refer to previous project planning documents.

Aerobics

1. Use the action steps matrix format to lay out tasks and responsibilities to meet milestones in the project. Emphasize actions between team decision points to get the necessary input and involvement of key stakeholders and stakeholder groups.

2. Do a force field analysis (see the separate tool sheet) to determine actions to break through barriers and to strengthen supporting elements in the environment. List the barriers (restraining forces) and helpers (driving forces). Under the barriers and helpers, list the actions the team decides on as the output of the force field work. (See Direction Exercise 7.)

3. List any resources and support needed to complete tasks and responsibilities and to make sure the drivers and restrainers are being addressed. (See Direction Exercise 6.)

4. Predict any issues/changes that are likely to pose problems or slow progress downstream (in the near future).

5. Check to make sure you have planned for adequate involvement of your key stakeholders to sufficiently address issues/concerns surfaced in aerobics steps 2, 3, and 4.

Cooldown

This framework can be used over and over again to update project planning. You might want to end this meeting with an open time for any team member to bring up remaining questions or concerns before moving into action.

High-Involvement Planning Guide

Project Description	Desired Outcomes

Action Steps

What	How	Who	When	Milestones

Driving Forces ————————————→ ←———————————— Restraining Forces

-
-
-

Resources/Support Needed

Need to have   *Nice* to have

Downstream Change Process Issues

DIRECTION EXERCISE 6
Resource Analysis

Workout Plan

When to use
When you need to identify the skills, talents, experience, resources, and networks needed to support team success and take an inventory of what the team possesses, as well as what the team may need from the outside.

When the team has come to agreement on its vision and mission or purpose and has a clear idea of the deliverables expected, use this exercise to determine what is required to achieve the desired results.

Time
One to two hours

Materials
Several packs of 3 × 5 white index cards, colored index cards for headers, markers, big blank wall space, and masking tape, if face-to-face.

If remote, use the worksheet provided and fax to a central location to be collated, or place the worksheets in the team's common computer database.

Purpose/objectives
- To identify strengths and gaps in the resources the team has immediately available to use in its work

- To plan for how to fill the gaps in order to ensure project success

Warm-up

If doing this in a face-to-face meeting, build a matrix on the wall like the worksheet shown, using masking tape for lines and writing headings on cards. Ask each team member to do an individual analysis for each category and post it on the wall. Make sure that only one idea is written on each card, and write with big markers so that the writing can be easily seen. If using a computer from various locations, give team members instructions and a deadline for providing input to the database.

Aerobics

1. Team members review aloud the cards they put onto the matrix while others listen, or all members review what is in the database.

2. Interactively look for areas that are well covered. List these as team strengths and identify some champions within the team that others can use as resources.

3. Identify gap areas where needs have been determined. You will know these because there is no match of strengths on the team. Brainstorm how to locate outside sources the team can tap to fill those gaps.

4. Create an action plan for contacting the outside sources and briefing them on the project and the possible need for their involvement. Use your team's project plan (such as your purpose statement) to help them see the need and get excited about helping to achieve your goals.

Cooldown

Make sure that each team member gets a list of resource people and their areas of strength.

Resource Planning Worksheet

	Needs	Strengths	Gaps	Actions
Skills—What competencies in team members can be applied to project goals and objectives?				
Talents—What special styles, personality traits, preferences, other interests could be tapped?				
Experience—Where have team members experienced similar situations? What best practices/worst practices should be considered?				
Resources—What materials, time, money, equipment will be needed?				
Network—Who outside the team could offer any of these? How can we include them?				

DIRECTION EXERCISE 7
Force Field Analysis

Workout Plan

When to use
When you need an accurate view of the current environment in which the project is occurring. Shows the existing forces that will *help* and those that will *hinder* the team as it tries to reach project results.

Time
One hour

Materials
Flip chart, masking tape, and markers if face-to-face
Shared database if remote
Force Field Analysis worksheet if phone conference

Purpose/objectives

- To analyze driving forces so that the team can plan actions that reinforce or strengthen them; also, to analyze inhibitors or restrainers so that the team can plan actions to minimize or neutralize them

- To understand the internal/external forces that promote or block effectiveness and progress

- To help the team work actively to overcome barriers, maximize promoters, and think creatively about how to ensure project success

- To provide a starting point for actions to take

Warm-up

On the shared database or (if face-to-face) on the wall or flip chart, draw a force field analysis diagram. Label the left side "driving forces" and the right side "restraining forces."

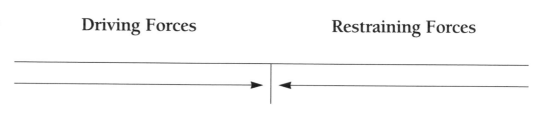

Driving Forces   **Restraining Forces**

Aerobics

1. Brainstorm the driving forces in existence that are working in favor of your goal. List these on the left side of the chart.

2. Brainstorm the restraining forces in place that are likely to get in the way of achieving the goal. List these on the right side of the chart.

3. Optional: Discuss and rank to identify the top four to five forces on each side that are most critical to your project.

4. Brainstorm solutions to minimize the major constraining forces and to maximize the promoting forces.

5. Plan action steps to take to ensure success.

Cooldown

Be sure to keep this work so that it can be reviewed periodically and updated.

Note: To be listed appropriately, forces must be those that already exist in the environment, not things that would help or hinder if they *were* put in place. This is not a decision-making tool where you list pros and cons. Once a decision on a goal is made, a force field analysis can help identify those forces that help or hinder implementation.

Force Field Analysis Worksheet

Chart the factors that are helping or promoting your efforts as well as those that are hindering you or restraining you. Prioritize each and determine actions to build promoters and minimize restrainers.

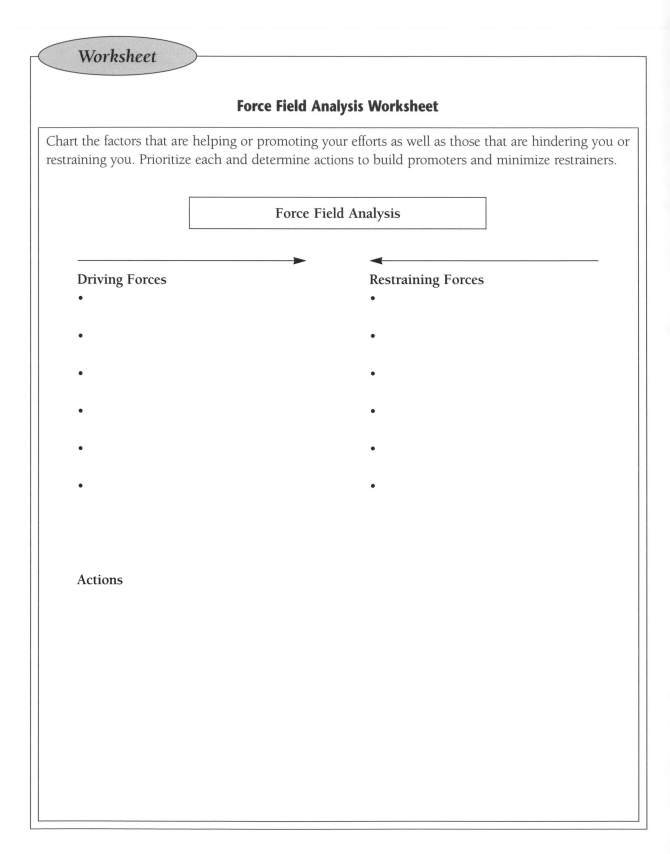

Force Field Analysis

Driving Forces

-
-
-
-
-
-

Restraining Forces

-
-
-
-
-
-

Actions

DIRECTION EXERCISE 8
Early Work Checklist

Workout Plan

When to use
When the project team is laying out objectives and creating the project plan/road map. This would be an appropriate activity at the end of the team start-up meeting. It would also work well in the first remote meeting after the team has started its work.

Time
Thirty minutes

Materials
Early Work Checklist worksheet
Project plans in their current draft stage

Purpose/objectives

- To ensure that during the early planning stages of the project, specific plans are made to allow for project progress to be tracked and measured

- To show what has changed versus what was in place before the project began

Warm-up

Team members rate the nine checkpoint statements on the checklist individually from 1 to 10, with 10 being the highest rating. If face-to-face, ratings are collected and displayed. If done by fax, one collection point is designated for collating ratings and the display is faxed back to all members before the conference meeting. If using a common database, members add their own ratings to the database and all review the collected ratings.

Aerobics

1. As a team, compare ratings to determine what points still need work or where there is confusion about what is in place.

2. Determine actions needed to get the necessary foundation in place and plan for those actions, as shown in the action box.

Cooldown

It is important that each action planning session end with specific responsibilities and commitments to enable team members to act on the team's behalf between meetings. All members should receive a copy of the action plan.

Early Work Checklist

On Track	Find Out	Needs Work	
			1. Objectives are stated in concrete measurable terms.
			2. Objectives have been translated into observable behaviors.
			3. Milestones are understood and agreed to.
			4. Expected results are tied to our team's goals and organizational goals.
			5. Stakeholders will see the results of our outcomes.
			6. Both individuals and teams are accountable for results.
			7. We can identify the data that show progress toward our goal.
			8. New ways to gather data are in place.
			9. We have accurate, up-to-date baseline data to work from.

Actions		
What	Who	When

Challenge 2: Values/Principles, Operating Agreements

Successful virtual teams have a set of values or principles and operating agreements that carry team members and leaders through the rough spots. While team members are autonomous, they also know what kinds of decisions to make, what methods to use for consistency, and how to support other team members.

VALUES STATEMENTS AND OPERATING AGREEMENTS ARE DEVELOPED UP FRONT

Many virtual teams have formal values statements that members agree to uphold when they join the team, whether they are permanently hired or temporarily assigned to a team or project. Agreements do not stop with the value statement, but take the statement and spell out the behaviors that would support or not

Operating agreements are made up front.

support the value for the particular work of the team. They also include a rationale of understanding why the value is important to the team's work.

Teams frequently devise a set of operating agreements based on the organization's or the team's values. These include such things as meeting deadlines, attendance at teleconferences, where decisions will be made by the whole team or by individuals, how to honor commitments to other team members, how to give each other bad news, specific roles and responsibilities, and expectations around communications.

Assumptions, expectations, roles, procedures, standards, norms, and processes must be explicit. If members make assumptions based on past experience without a clear definition among teammates, time and effort can be wasted. Once the agreements are clear and in place, they enhance the development of a common language, helping team members work with a minimum of misunderstandings.

Operating Agreements—Example

Each team member will be expected to

- **Demonstrate a realistic understanding of his or her role and accountabilities.**

- **Use objective and fact-based judgments.**

- **Collaborate effectively with other team members.**

- **Make the team goal a higher priority than any personal objective.**

- **Devote whatever effort is necessary to achieve team success.**

- **Be willing to share information, perceptions, and feedback openly.**

- **Provide help to other team members when needed and as appropriate.**

- **Work to high standards of excellence.**

- **Demonstrate courage of conviction by directly confronting important issues.**

- **Provide leadership that contributes to the team's success.**

- **Respond constructively to feedback from others.**

Source: Larson and LaFasto 1989, 124

BASIC METHODOLOGIES MUST ALSO BE CLEAR

All teams use basic methods such as problem solving, decision making, conflict management, and technology applications. When a team agrees on the "five steps of problem solving" or the "three phases to working through a conflict," a great deal of time in working together is saved. These agreements on methodology become a common language and context that triggers understanding in remote communication. An example of this sort of agreement for structuring meetings is shown in appendix C.

Team norms can be anything that team members feel is important for everyone to commit to doing. For instance, one item might be that everyone checks into the database once a day to monitor the progress of the project, even if she has no new information to add. Other norms might deal with the way information is handled. Which kinds of issues are discussed by the team as a whole, and how often? Does everyone have access to all information, or is some of it restricted?

Other agreed-upon practices might cover ways to deal with conflict. Teams sometimes enforce a rule that if one team member has a conflict with another and it can't be dealt with electronically, then they must telephone or meet in person.

Chris Newell
Lotus Institute
(Geber 1995, 40)

TEAMS DECIDE HOW TO USE THE VARIOUS TECHNOLOGIES AVAILABLE

A fundamental distinction between dispersed teams and co-located teams is their reliance on technological means of working together.

Culture, leadership, and learning will help define the way the group uses the technology. The existence of a common language is critical. For instance, when one team member refers to a specific computer application, a certain image and terminology instantly comes to mind with others. If teams can receive similar training in the applications they use and can be open about the way they want to use the technology and the norms around its use, they can gel and get to results quickly.

At Price Waterhouse, some virtual teams work together for just a week or two, preparing a project for a particular client. Sheldon Laube, National Director of Information and Technology, says, "It would be unrealistic to put everyone on a plane for a get-together when all the necessary information can be coalesced quickly on networked computers." Considering that Price Waterhouse has 45,000 employees in 120 countries, people often work on projects without benefit of having met in person. But Laube maintains that the company's set methodology and common language for conducting audits eases collaboration. He also adds that there is a strong expectation within the company that colleagues share information freely with one another.

Source: Geber 1995, 38

GROUP CULTURE DEVELOPS AS THE TEAM WORKS TOGETHER

When I worked at StorageTek, our training and organization development department had a wonderful ground rule. You were expected to collaborate with someone in the department on team building design, course development, or other important matters. If you approached another member of the team and asked for advice or counsel, they would freely give it. You did not have to accept the advice, but if you chose to do so and it didn't work, it was not the fault of the advisor. It was still your problem.

Jane E. Henry, coauthor

The agreements that are made early on will need to be revisited as the project gets started and new norms evolve. Virtual teams, like other teams, go through stages of forming, norming, storming, and performing. If this process is left to chance, even a strong start can be lost as new situations and complexities appear.

SUMMARY

The challenge facing virtual teams is the possibility of misunderstanding and conflict. If team members can work together up front to develop their own norms and expectations based on team and organizational values, they can do much to maximize their potential to produce effective results. Clarifying your team's values and principles is introspective and specific for each team. In the following exercises you'll see several approaches to this work. Choose the ones you believe your team will be most responsive to.

VALUES/PRINCIPLES EXERCISE 1
What Values for Our Team?

Workout Plan

When to use
When the team is trying to determine the values that should be explicitly shared by team members and used to guide decisions and actions of the team.

Time
One to two hours

Materials
Possible Outcomes worksheet. The first step, generating and gathering ideas, can easily be done face-to-face, by fax, or on a database. The discussion and decision making that follows can be done in a conference meeting, but it is preferable to do this face-to-face as values are deeply held and it is the quality of the discussion that makes them truly shared among team members.

Purpose/objectives
- To create a mind-set of the kinds of values that are special and particular to the work of the team

- To avoid "apple pie and motherhood" values and, instead, pick those that really count

Warm-up
Each team member should come to the meeting (in-person or conference meeting) having filled out the Possible Outcomes worksheet.

Aerobics

1. Go around the team, round-robin (one at a time), and ask each team member to suggest a value for the team and talk about how it will help avoid the "worst possible outcome" or how it will help make the "best possible outcome" come true. List each value as it is suggested.

2. Discuss the values as a group. Which seem to stand out most to team members? Which do they feel are most critical?

3. Narrow the list if needed. A team should not have more than a "handful" of values so that it can easily remember them and work from them.

Cooldown

The values chosen should pass the following acid test.

1. Does each value represent an important aspect of how the team works? Is it central to success—a real "need to have," rather than "nice to have"?

2. Taken together, do the values seem sufficient—do they cover the major areas that could make or break the team? (This is a good time to go back to your initial project plans to see if the values are related.)

3. Do the proposed values represent the kind of team each member would truly be proud to be a part of?

Possible Outcomes Worksheet

As you think of project results, what are the

Worst possible outcomes

_____

_____

_____

_____

_____

Best possible outcomes

_____

_____

_____

_____

_____

Values that will help ensure achieving the best possible outcomes and avoiding the worst

_____

_____

_____

_____

_____

VALUES/PRINCIPLES EXERCISE 2
Testing the Values

Workout Plan

When to use
When the team has brainstormed a list of possible values and wants a mechanism to help decide which values are critical to live by. This is also useful to determine meaning for each value so that expectations are clearly known to team members.

Time
One to two hours

Materials
Brainstormed list of values
Testing the Values worksheet for individual use

Although this exercise can be done remotely, it is best done face-to-face in the team start-up meeting.

Purpose/objectives
- To spell out the specific behaviors that would "live out" each value

- To make clear what the team would expect from each team member if a particular value were adopted

Warm-up

If you have not already brainstormed a list of potential values to guide the work of the team, do that now to begin the activity. Use consensus or simply check the three or four values each team member sees as most critical to find the several where there is agreement. From that, determine the handful of values that seem to be most important to adopt.

Aerobics

1. Assign a pair or threesome to consider several of the chosen values so that for each value you have two groups assigned to describe it. Ask groups to fill out the Testing the Values worksheet, showing particular behaviors for the team that would discourage, allow, or actively show the adoption of the value.

2. Bring the drafts done in small groups back to the whole team. (If you are doing this remotely, have all groups enter their work in the common database.)

3. As an entire team, review the drafts for each value, adding and editing as the team feels the need to.

4. When all values have been reviewed, decide which will become the guideposts for the team. Allow adequate time to discuss them before decisions are made. Everyone can agree on "motherhood and apple pie" values, but to have meaning, the values should address the complexities and dilemmas the team will face. Getting together on values at this deeper level takes time and a clear understanding of what each value means to actions.

Cooldown

The values chosen should pass the following acid test.

1. Does each value chosen represent an important aspect of how the team works? Is it central to success—a real "need to have," rather than "nice to have"?

2. Taken together, do the values seem sufficient—do they cover the major areas that could make or break the team? (This is a good time to go back to your critical success factors to see if the values are related.)

3. Do the proposed values represent the team each member would truly be proud to be a part of?

Example

Value: Teamwork—Working with others in such a way that the sum is more than the parts.

Thinking/rationale: We live in a fast-paced world, where customer demands and needs often change. We can achieve better results and meet these needs when we work together instead of as individuals.

Behaviors: Asking for and giving help. "What do you think?" "How can I help?" Identifying others who can help with a problem and offering what you have to help solve it. Acknowledging the work of others. Saying thanks. Offering assistance to someone in another department. Holding the group mutually accountable for goals. Coaching each other.

Testing the Values Worksheet

Example:

Value = Doing excellent work through continuous improvement of all products and processes

Behaviors That *Ignore* Continuous Improvement
• Cancel several problem-solving meetings: This says clearly that continuous improvement is not as important as other things.
• Meet the deadline in spite of problems that affect quality: This says that schedule is more important than excellent work.

Behaviors That *Allow* Continuous Improvement
• Hold occasional group meetings with subordinates to explain some techniques for continuous improvement: This is not "continuous, gentle, relentless" pressure, but rather it says we do this when there is time.
• Distribute literature on quality: No follow-up action is indicated.

Behaviors That *Live* Continuous Improvement
• Commend several subordinates during staff meeting for personally pitching in to make improvements: This shows the importance of quality improvement.
• Review improvement efforts at the beginning of each staff meeting: This puts the emphasis on quality on a day-to-day basis.

Value: _____

Behaviors that show we *ignore* our value:

_____
_____
_____
_____
_____

Behaviors that *allow* the value, but are neutral:

_____
_____
_____
_____
_____

Behaviors that show we *live* our value, even when it is difficult:

_____
_____
_____
_____
_____

VALUES/PRINCIPLES EXERCISE 3
What Do Our Values Mean?

Workout Plan

When to use
When the team has brainstormed a list of possible values and wants a mechanism to help decide which are critical to live by. This is also useful as a way to determine meaning for each value so that each team member is clear about expected behaviors.

Time
One to two hours

Materials
Brainstormed list of values
Describing the Values worksheet for individual use

Although this exercise can be done remotely, it would be best done face-to-face in the team start-up meeting.

Purpose/objectives
- To spell out the behaviors that would "live out" each value

- To make clear what the team would expect from each team member if a particular value were adopted

Warm-up

Ask team members to pair up (in person or on the phone) and decide two values they both agree are critical for team success. Have them use the Describing the Values worksheet to help ensure that they are talking about values with the same or similar meaning.

Aerobics

1. Each pair gets together (in person or on the phone) with a second pair, and they compare the values generated in their original pairs. The foursome decides which values they wish to propose to the entire team.

2. The team meets (in person or by videoconference) and the foursomes presents the values they believe are important, making sure they thoroughly explain the rationale and behaviors that give meaning to each value.

3. The whole team determines what handful (five to seven) of values to put in place that everyone agrees are important to the success of the team. Adequate time for discussion should be taken before decisions are made. Everyone can agree on "motherhood and apple pie" values, but to have meaning, the values should address the complexities and dilemmas the team will face. Agreement on values at this deeper level takes time and a clear understanding of what each value means in action.

Cooldown

The values chosen should pass the following acid test.

1. Does each value chosen represent an important aspect of how the team works? Is it central to success—a real "need to have," rather than "nice to have"?

2. Taken together, do the values seem sufficient—do they cover the major areas that could make or break the team? (This is a good time to go back to your initial project plans to see if the values are related.)

3. Do the proposed values represent the team each member would truly be proud to be a part of?

Describing the Values Worksheet

> **Behaviors**
> How would we see ourselves living the value?
> How could others know our beliefs by watching us?
>
> > **Thinking/Rationale**
> > The rationale—Why is our belief important to our success?
> >
> > > **Values**
> > > What we believe that will guide our teamwork

Directions: Create a rationale and suggest behaviors for each value you want for the team.

Value: _____

Thinking/Rationale: _____

_____

_____

_____

_____

_____

Behaviors: _____

_____

_____

_____

_____

_____

_____

_____

_____

_____

VALUES/PRINCIPLES EXERCISE 4
The Origin of My Values

Workout Plan

When to use
When the team is forming and wants to clarify its values and decide on those that will be used to guide the team's behavior.

Time
One to two hours

Materials
Flip chart paper or database to record themes. Although this exercise can be done remotely, it would be best accomplished in a face-to-face team meeting.

Purpose/objectives
- To help team members get at their deepest values and share them with other team members

- To look for commonalities and differences among team members

- To connect personal values to those that will best serve the team

Warm-up
Explain that some literature claims that many closely held values are formed by the time we are 10 years old. In order to look at those long-term values, we will do a guided recall that will help individuals remember their world at the age of 10.

Aerobics

1. The leader or facilitator will give the following instructions and ask the questions, allowing at least two minutes between questions. Ask team members to relax and think back to the time they were ten. They may want to close their eyes and drift back in time.

   - What year was it?

   - Where did you live?

   - What was your house like?

   - Who else lived in the house?

   - What did your parents do for a living?

   - Where did you go to school?

   - What was your school like?

   - What did you do for fun?

   - Who were your heroes?

   - What were the headlines in the paper?

   - What did you want to be when you grew up?

2. After everyone has had the chance to think about these questions, go around round-robin (one at a time) and ask people to share something they remembered. Others may want to take some notes.

3. Look for the themes and commonalities. What were some of the differences?

4. How have the themes shaped and affected the way people on the team behave and believe?

5. What values stem from these themes?

6. What values for the work of the team could be drawn from those strongly held individual values?

Cooldown

Ask members to share one way they believe the individual values expressed will be important to and contribute to the team's success.

VALUES/PRINCIPLES EXERCISE 5
Decision Grid

Workout Plan

When to use
When determining how team members will be involved in various project decisions.

Time
One to one and a half hours

Materials
Decision Making Grid worksheet. If doing this remotely, each team member can fill out the grid independently, then ratings can be collected and collated. Then in the team conference meeting, the discussion hinges on getting to a common understanding in those areas where team members did not initially agree.

Purpose/objectives
- To enhance team buy-in by developing a decision-making protocol

- To clarify in advance each member's involvement in key decisions so that there are no surprises during the project work

Warm-up
Brainstorm and prioritize a list of key decisions that the team will make for their work.

Aerobics

1. Place each member's name on the left side of the grid. Place key decision issues across the top of the grid.

2. Work through the grid point by point, determining each person's involvement. Discuss the rationale behind each agreement made so that team members develop an overall understanding of how and why certain types of decisions will be made.

3. Check for agreement and understanding as you go.

Cooldown

Make sure that the rationale for decisions also gets recorded in a more general way—for example, "most staffing decisions made by team leader and two project managers"—so that the principles used can be applied to later situations as well.

Decision Grid Worksheet

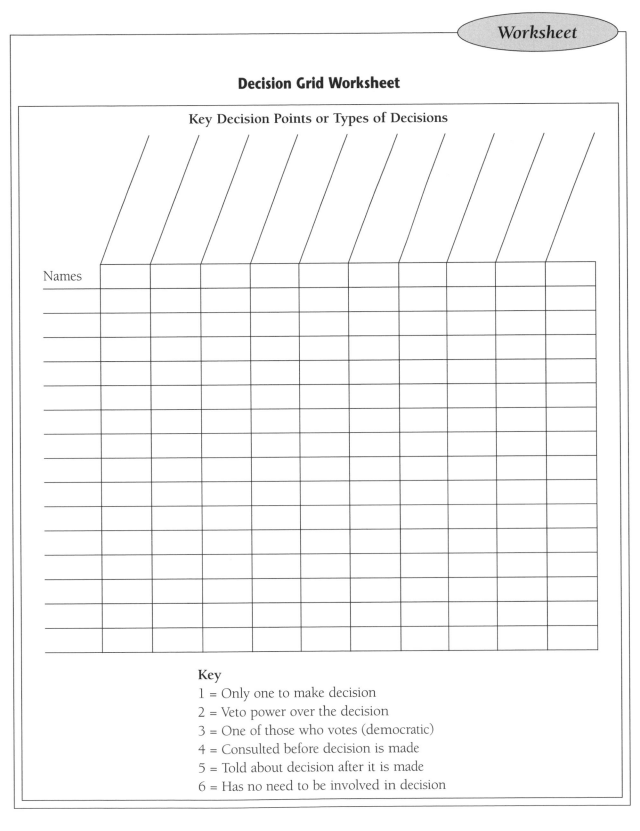

Key Decision Points or Types of Decisions

Names

Key

1 = Only one to make decision

2 = Veto power over the decision

3 = One of those who votes (democratic)

4 = Consulted before decision is made

5 = Told about decision after it is made

6 = Has no need to be involved in decision

VALUES/PRINCIPLES EXERCISE 6
Team Operating Agreements

Workout Plan

When to use
When the team is forming—before there are confusions, or before different ways of operating causes problems. Operating agreements also frequently evolve over time and can be revised or added to at any time when the need becomes apparent.

Time
One to two hours

Materials
Flip chart paper and markers if face-to-face
Operating Agreements worksheet when working face-to-face or remote

Purpose/objectives
- To specify the behaviors the team agrees to use or not to use

- To serve as a contract between team members on issues critical to team effectiveness

- To give members the responsibility and the means to work through tensions or issues that arise between team members

- To prevent conflicts and surprises

Warm-up

Decide on some of the areas that should be covered by operating agreements for the team. You can use the suggestions listed here as a starting place. Remember that many of the exercises in this book result in agreements that become part of your team's operating agreements.

Aerobics

1. Discuss the need or use of operating agreements (use the purposes suggested).

2. Draft an appropriate agreement for each area you have chosen in the warm-up. This can be done in small groups with each group drafting an agreement for one area, or it can be done as a complete team.

3. Circulate copies of the drafts, or review and discuss them one by one.

4. Come to consensus on the final agreement in each area. You may need to test the agreements before members will know if they are appropriate. You can test by giving examples of what would meet the agreement or what would go against the agreement. You can also determine how to handle it when an agreement is broken. If you go through this step, your agreements will be much stronger. Add one hour to complete it in this fashion.

Suggested topics for operating agreements for virtual teams

- How and when to conduct meetings

- How decisions will be made and with whose involvement

- How feedback on work will be given

- How bad news will be delivered to other team members

- Agreements around deadlines and milestones

- How to keep everyone informed

- Methods for acknowledging receipt of information

- Upkeep and updating of databases

- How to ask for and receive help

- Expectations between team members and the team leader

- How to ensure there is fun and celebration are built into the process

- Handling confidentiality

Cooldown

Distribute copies of agreements to each team member. Plan to check in regular meetings the degree to which members are—or are not—living up to the agreements made. These operating agreements are also used to help new team members know and understand the culture and expectations of the team.

VALUES/PRINCIPLES EXERCISE 7
Customer Operating Agreements

Workout Plan

When to use
When the team has developed initial plans. If an early customer meeting is planned, this activity is especially appropriate. If one team member is the customer contact, the team may develop a draft for that member to work from when meeting with the customer. Either way, it is critical that the customer is part of performing this activity.

Time
One hour

Materials
Flip chart paper and markers if face-to-face

Purpose/objectives
- To specify the behaviors the team and customer agree to use or not to use as they work together

- To serve as a contract between team members and the customer on issues critical to meeting the customer's needs

- To give members the responsibility and the means to work through tensions or issues that occur between the team and its customers

- To prevent conflicts and surprises

Warm-up

Decide on some of the areas that should be covered by operating agreements with the customer. You can use the suggestions listed here as a starting place.

Aerobics

1. Discuss the need or use of operating agreements (use the purposes suggested).

2. Draft an appropriate agreement for each area you have chosen in the warm-up. This can be done in small groups with each group drafting an agreement for one area, or it can be done as a whole team.

3. Circulate copies of the drafts or review and discuss them one by one.

4. Come to consensus on the final agreement in each area. You may need to test the agreements before members will know if they are appropriate. You can test by giving examples of what would meet the agreement or what would go against the agreement. You can also determine how to handle it when an agreement is broken.

Suggested topics for customer operating agreements for virtual teams

- Scope of work

- Expected results

- Processes/methods

- Required information and resources

- Ways to communicate

- Deliverables and schedule

- Roles

- Wants and offers for how to treat each other

Cooldown

Plan with the customer for process checks in your meetings to determine how well agreements are or are not being followed.

Challenge 3: Synergy/Communication

Perhaps the greatest challenge to a virtual team is how to keep the synergy and creativity flowing without day-to-day interaction. Keeping the momentum going can be difficult in any situation, but virtual teams find this to be especially difficult because of their dispersed locations. Communication is the vehicle for creating the synergy, keeping the team together, and moving forward.

Virtual teams are required to overcommunicate. Team leaders find they must be much more deliberate and structured in their coordination efforts. Many kinds of technologies are used to keep the team together and in alignment. Teams communicate regularly by telephone, fax, videoconferencing, shared databases, and a myriad of technologies. The challenge is to create effective communications across the miles.

COMMUNICATION IS MORE STRUCTURED THAN IN CO-LOCATED TEAMS

Communication is most frequently related to the tasks and progress of the team. In organizations that have an informal mode of management and communication, the leader or coordinator has to pay extra attention to the deliberate, defined communication and ways to make sure there is consistency and understanding.

Overcommunicate. Use fax, video conferencing, the Internet, the telephone—whatever it takes.

In addition, the communication must flow two ways. When information is sent, it must be acknowledged so that it isn't lost in cyberspace. Nothing can be left to chance. As one leader put it, "You can't assume anything."

If members need feedback on some idea or project, they must ask for it specifically. One can't just say, "Tell me what you think." Rather, say something like, "What do you think about this particular idea? What if we did this? Look at page 2, line 24. Is that correct?"

THERE IS NO QUICK FIX FOR MISCOMMUNICATION

If people don't know each other well, communications can easily be interpreted incorrectly. Conflict has a tendency to escalate when there is no opportunity to stop by someone's office and ask "What did you mean by that?" to clear up misunderstandings immediately. Miscommunication may simmer and erupt at an unforeseen time, causing consternation and surprise.

On the positive side, however, some people report that conflict on dispersed teams is minimized because the anonymity of the technological methods of communication leads to a lack of hierarchical status and domination by those with more forceful personalities.

DIVERSITY AND CROSS-CULTURAL DIFFERENCES MUST BE DEALT WITH

Differences can occur in body language, slang, or in-house ways of talking to each other, as well as the more obvious forms such as speaking different languages. Differences also occur between corporate and field sites, site cultures, geo-

> Conditions that promote greater understanding and linking between cultural groups are equality, superordinate goals, frequent contact, and mutual knowledge.
>
> *Source:* Armstrong and Cole 1995, 212

graphic locations, and between countries and nationalities. Teams must find a common means to work through different ways of expressing issues and ideas.

INFORMAL INTERACTION MUST BE BUILT INTO THE TEAM'S EVERYDAY AGENDA

Communications are time-consuming; plus you have differences in language, cross-cultural understanding, and time zones. Teleconference conversations may be too formal. It can be hard even to reach someone when you need them.

Judy Issokson
Program Manager, Management Development
Sun Microsystems

Sometimes decisions are made in subgroups, without the whole team being involved. Members and leaders have to consciously and consistently work to keep all members informed. The logic involved in those decisions is especially important for those who are not part of the everyday interactions of their colleagues. Effort needs to be made to keep members involved in "hallway chats." Some good team leaders intentionally

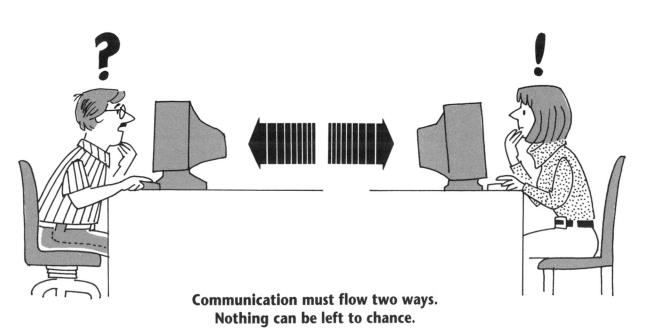

Communication must flow two ways.
Nothing can be left to chance.

"bump into their members on the telephone" on a personal basis as well as on a task basis. A "huddle" by chat room or teleconference is a good way to keep up involvement. At the huddle, everyone quickly checks on progress toward a particular project or goal. The huddle is informal and quick. Because of time differences and scheduling difficulties, it is best to try to set a specific time each week to "huddle."

Involving all sites in a teleconference meeting requires discipline and patience. "Off-site, out of mind," is an easy mistake to make. Not only is it easy to forget to tell remote sites of changes, it is also easy to disregard their input during teleconferencing. If most of the people are located at one site, teleconferences can become one-way communication devices rolling over and ignoring the input from remote sites. We have even seen the mute button pushed while the dominant site discusses issues without involving the whole team.

Perhaps the group, in its discussion of team norms, should talk about when and how to bring up tentative new ideas and approaches— the kind of things that normally would get talked about in hallway chats, the lunchroom, or the coffee room.

TEAMS NEED MULTIPLE COMMUNICATION TECHNOLOGIES

In addition to face-to-face meetings that enhance communication and understanding, various technologies are used to keep members informed and involved. Regular teleconferencing helps. Videoconferencing, although more expensive and not always available, allows team members to see each other and read body language. Shared databases, if updated and read on a regular basis, keep members current on project progress. Faxes, telephone calls, and voice messaging can clear up problems quickly. Email to all members or to individual members is speedy and keeps the channels of communication operative.

MUTUAL TRUST IS IMPORTANT

The need to build trust with people you don't know well is intensified. People like to know the whole person, the broader personality. Trust comes from working together to solve problems and getting energy from fellow team members. Communication for virtual teams is generally more structured and task oriented. Therefore, some of the excitement and energy from working as a team can be lost between the widely separated locations.

DISPERSED TEAMS CAN DEVELOP THEIR OWN CULTURES AND RITUALS

One evening I was working late with a group of clients on a teleconference call. We were all tired and a little stressed. The fax machine was making its usual grinding noises. Suddenly, the office door opened and a man delivered my favorite pizza. I was amazed! It had come from my colleagues on the call, who were also having pizza. When I looked over to the fax machine, it was sending out pictures of pizzas of all kinds. We laughed, enjoyed our meal, and soon regained our energy to finish our business.

Meg Hartzler, coauthor

It is difficult for virtual teams to replicate the hallway chats, the family talk, and inside jokes, and to find reasons and ways to pull together. An effective way to develop a team culture is to meet at various sites throughout the team's life. Then while the team meets electronically, each can picture the other members at their own site.

Rituals of initiation can also help break down barriers. Sometimes teams bring songs, beverages, or folk art that are representative of their home site to group meetings, or share something specific to their locale in the warm-up to the meeting.

TEAM MEMBERS BENEFIT FROM KNOWING EACH OTHER ON A PERSONAL, SOCIAL BASIS

Synergy and creativity are central reasons for working in teams. These elements are more difficult to build and sustain for dispersed teams.

> Susan McPherson, CEO of Creative Communications Consultants, invited her freelance "creatives" to join agency staff for the company's annual family picnic at her home in Minnesota. "The energy was wonderful. We now have a broader, fuller relationship. We don't just relate on the task level. Now we have a bigger picture of the people. Creatives talk to each other, energize each other, like to learn from each other."

One of the solutions to this difficulty is to bring members together in a social situation at the beginning of a project and at certain times throughout the project. Investment in this activity, as part of the project, helps to promote creativity and synergy.

> **T**he hardest thing is the lack of the micro-interactions. Magic comes in the oddest places—chance remarks, the lame joke, walking to the restaurant for a sandwich. It's hard to fabricate the pressure cooker without the interactions. I manage chemistry. I can leverage the best talent all over the world. We have to find the magic, the creative spirit.
>
> **John Coleman**
> **President**
> **ViA Marketing & Design**

Other teams get together for ski weekends, barbecues, or sporting events. Leaders report that these fun times build trust, understanding, and good memories that last a long time, bridging the usual miles between team members. Sometimes they become the glue that holds the team together.

Managing the magic of a virtual team is a difficult, but rewarding, job.

VIRTUAL TEAM LEADERS AND MEMBERS MUST HAVE STAMINA AND ENDURANCE

People want answers to their questions when they need them. Because virtual teams often inhabit different time zones, the problem a member is dealing with at noon can be at the end of the day or the middle of the night for another member. Outlying team members run into frustration at not being able to reach the leader or other team members when needed. herefore, agreements must be reached early in the formation of the team about what is critical and what can wait.

Tips for Teleconference Meetings

1. Send out the agenda and supplemental reading ahead of time.

2. Agree ahead of time about how to handle absences.

3. Start on time.

4. Begin with a roll call. Add something personal as a warm-up to bring people mentally, if not physically, together. This can be something about the weather, business conditions in their locale, fast-breaking news, upcoming company events, and so on.

5. Review the agenda and ask for comments.

6. Use some method of recording key comments and decisions for each agenda item. Use this summary to check for agreement and understanding before moving to the next item.

7. Rotate the order in which you poll members.

8. End with a process check of meeting effectiveness.

9. Ask members to summarize discussions and decisions that were made.

10. Set a time for the next conference and check for agenda items that are already known or are carryovers from this meeting.

11. Follow up immediately with written minutes.

Additional Tips for Videoconferencing

Videoconferencing is relatively expensive, has a scheduled time that must be adhered to, and requires a certain amount of discipline to stay with the agenda, prioritize, and discuss the most important topics.

It offers the advantage of seeing people's reactions to various issues and more closely resembles a face-to-face meeting than other forms of communication. Follow the advice given for teleconferencing. Additionally, the following tips apply.

1. Ask questions to get participation.

2. Pause long enough for answers. There may be a slight delay in the transfer of images. Allow the on-screen site to finish speaking before you respond.

3. Use graphics. Keep them large and simple.

4. Be yourself. Speak naturally, as if you were all in a room together.

5. Be aware of which camera you are using.

6. Tell people when you will be using a graphic.

7. Avoid wearing white, red, plaids, or print clothes.

8. Summarize the discussion and decisions, visually if possible.

SUMMARY

Managing the synergy of a virtual team is a difficult but rewarding job. The leader has access to the finest talents to bring to bear on the problem or project. Striving to create the personal, energetic side of team membership in a calculated, deliberate fashion can make the difference between ordinary and extraordinary results.

Communication can be more difficult with dispersed teams, but new vistas can open up through the use of various technologies

> When we finish a conference call, video or audio, each participant is asked what they heard, what was agreed to. Then follow-up is made immediately with written communication to prevent any misunderstandings.
>
> **Richard A. Gould**
> **Supplier Engineering**
> **Western Digital Corporation**

and a very structured formal and informal approach. These, when well planned and executed, will help ensure that each team member has what he or she needs to move ahead individually.

SYNERGY/COMMUNICATION EXERCISE 1
In-Depth Cross-Cultural Introductions

Workout Plan

When to use
At any time during the team's life, but this is most effectively used in the beginning. This activity can be done by telephone, videoconference, computer, or face-to-face. Although this exercise seems to be based on differences between countries, it is also useful for different sites within the same country—for example, east-west, north-south, headquarters-field.

This exercise can be used effectively at the beginning of the development of operating agreements, to set the stage appropriately.

Time
One hour, more or less, depending on the number of questions selected and the number of members on the team

Materials
Send out the following in advance.

- A copy of the questions for each person

- A copy of the In-Depth Cross-Cultural Introductions worksheet for each person

Purpose/objectives
- To get to know each team member better

- To develop respect for each person's preferred methods of communication

- To prevent misunderstandings and conflict

Warm-up

Explain that there are no right or wrong answers to these questions. The purpose is simply to learn to understand each other better. The questions represent areas where there are usually the most cross-cultural differences between people. By learning how each of us likes to work, we can gain respect for each person's preferred methods of working with others. Hopefully we can also prevent misunderstandings and conflict.

Aerobics

1. Select the questions the team believes are most appropriate for the group from the suggestions offered.

2. Go around the team and have each person answer each question, one at a time.

3. Use the worksheet to make notes so that each member can concentrate on what is said and can remember the comments.

Suggested questions

- What are your expectations in the area of time frames? Do people in your culture believe that deadlines are requirements, options, or moving targets? Do you usually think in terms of the very long term, or more immediate short-term goals?

- Would you describe yourself as more action oriented, or thoughtful and reflective?

- How is it best to communicate to you? Written, verbal, other?

- Are suggestions viewed as calls for actions, food for thought, or directives?

- What is your philosophy toward people in positions of power? How do you tend to behave when working with people who have more power than you? Less power than you?

- What is the role of the individual in your culture? Do people tend to work alone, or prefer to work collectively?

- Do you find the people in your culture to be competitive? Or do they avoid competition? Is competition considered rude?

- Do you generally follow a hierarchical structure? Do you prefer to "go through the channels?" Or do you prefer to work with whomever you believe you need to in order to get the work accomplished?

- How do you prefer to work with others? Do you like to be more formal and polite? Or do you like to be casual and informal? What would be an example of rudeness or impropriety in this area?

Cooldown

Ask team members to summarize the most important ideas they heard. Were there certain areas in which they felt in complete agreement? Were there areas of clear-cut differences? What should the team do about those differences?

In-Depth Cross-Cultural Introductions

Team member's name	Time	Action	Preferred communication method

In-Depth Cross-Cultural Introductions *(continued)*

Suggestions	Power	Individual vs. collective	Hierarchy	Formality

SYNERGY/COMMUNICATION EXERCISE 2
Agenda Planning Format

Workout Plan

When to use
Use before each team meeting, whether face-to-face or remote. Also use within smaller groups of the team when groups meet for task work.

Time
30 to 60 minutes

Materials
Agenda worksheet

Purpose/objectives

- To ensure that each agenda item has been well planned

- To communicate clearly to all team members what the team should accomplish in the meeting

- To enhance meeting efficiency and effectiveness

- To gain input on agenda topics from all team members

Warm-up

One team member can draft the agenda and circulate it to others for review. Input to the agenda can be posted or entered on the shared database so that all team members can contribute agenda items. A draft can be faxed to each member for review and input. The key element is *input—each member* has an opportunity to influence what is placed on the agenda.

Aerobics

1. Collect agenda items.

2. Review carefully to make sure outcomes are not activities and that the approach and method are clearly written.

3. Determine the amount of time needed and who will lead the discussion for each agenda item.

4. Add any information needed for prework.

5. Distribute agenda and prework to team members for review.

6. Adjust and modify the agenda according to team member input (sometimes before and sometimes at the beginning of the meeting). Remember that the plan doesn't always work as designed. Be prepared to stop and renegotiate time spent on items as you go through the meeting.

Example

Sample Meeting Agenda				
Date:		**Time:**		**Place:**

Meeting purpose: To identify all key stakeholders for this project and create action plan to obtain buy-in.

Meeting outcome: A written action plan with names and accountabilities by stakeholder.

Topic/Area	Desired Outcome	Approach	Time	Who
Meeting purpose	Agreement	Presentation and Q&A	5 min.	
Review agenda	Agreement	Presentation and Q&A	3 min.	
Status update, project scope (why, what, when, where, how issues)	Group understands and has common knowledge of project	Presentation and Q&A	10 min.	
Identify key stakeholders ❑ Define term ❑ Identify categories ❑ Identify names	List of categories List of people ❑ Prioritized	Storyboard ❑ Cards filled out round-robin style ❑ Prioritize ❑ Check agreements	30 min.	
Commitment charting ❑ Top 10 people and others later	Identify where each person is and where they need to be	General discussion	15 min.	
Action plan— next steps	Someone is assigned to each stakeholder, next steps to take	Leader asks for volunteers for each stakeholder, group vote for consensus	20 min.	
			Total: 83 min.	

Cooldown

Some teams build or at least start to build the agenda for the next meeting as the last agenda item of each meeting. This helps to ensure that tabled items or new items generated during the meeting do not get dropped or lost.

Meeting Agenda Worksheet

❏ Team name
❏ Meeting purpose
❏ Date, time, location

Topic (What)	Desired Outcome/Product	Approach (How)	Time (How long)	Leader (Who)

SYNERGY/COMMUNICATION EXERCISE 3
Meeting Evaluation—Process Checks

Workout Plan

When to use
At the end of team meetings or important team events, such as customer meetings.

Time
Ten minutes to one hour

Materials
Choose one of the five worksheets.

Purpose/objectives
- To provide an opportunity for adjustments to keep the team on track

- To generate specific ideas about how to improve future meetings

- To build a habit of continuous improvement

- To build an atmosphere of candid discussion without blame

Warm-up
Choose the worksheet format you wish to follow. Ask team members to rate the meeting individually, using the Process Check worksheet you have chosen for guidance. If remote, you may need to do this verbally because you cannot collect the input ahead of time—it

depends on how you just ran the meeting. You can, however, make sure that team members have a hard copy of all formats and can review the one you wish to work from during the meeting.

Aerobics

1. Capture ratings or ideas from all team members, following the worksheet you have chosen.

2. Facilitate a discussion by

   - Summarizing observations on the distribution of ratings (is it a tight grouping or wide range?).

   - Asking for comments on the rationale for both high and low ratings.

   - Focusing attention by giving examples from the meeting regarding each topic.

   - Asking for specific behaviors. The ground rule for this activity is simply to listen to each person's perception, not to argue or explain. Each person gives his or her impressions, with no group evaluation of the impressions given.

3. Ask for specific ways future meetings can be improved and how to continue to emphasize the most successful aspects of the meeting.

4. List improvement ideas—only three or four.

Cooldown

Include ideas for improvement in the beginning of the next meeting to focus team members on effective actions.

Note: The focus should be on how to learn from the observations, not on the numerical ratings. If used consistently, in time this process will become a habit and team members will be less defensive about criticisms.

Process Check #1

1. Generally speaking, our meeting was

Disappointing	1 2 3 4 5 6 7	Great
Disjointed	1 2 3 4 5 6 7	Crisp
Lethargic	1 2 3 4 5 6 7	Energetic

_____

_____

_____

For our next meeting, we should

❑

2. Our process

Was unstructured	1 2 3 4 5 6 7	Was structured
Distracted us from the task	1 2 3 4 5 6 7	Facilitated our task
Was conflicted	1 2 3 4 5 6 7	Was cooperative

_____

_____

_____

For our next meeting, we should

❑

❑

Process Check #2

Directions: Brainstorm ideas, categorize and discuss, make agreements on changes or actions to take.

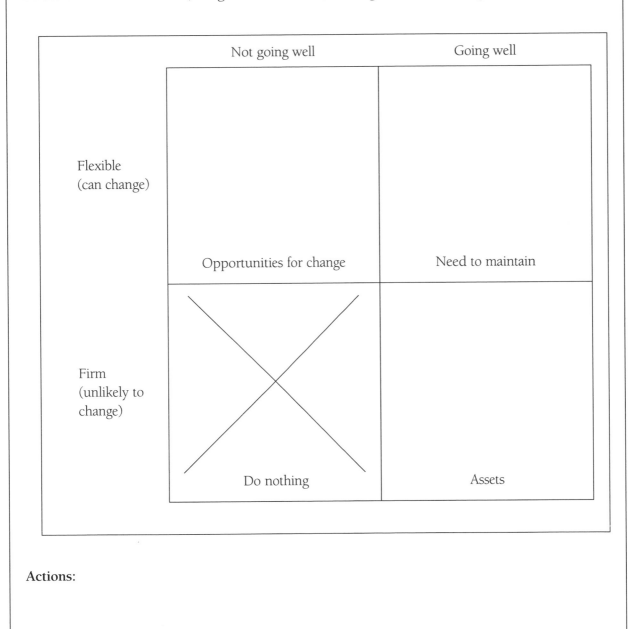

	Not going well	Going well
Flexible (can change)	Opportunities for change	Need to maintain
Firm (unlikely to change)	Do nothing	Assets

Actions:

Process Check #3

Brainstorm how your team can be more effective in conducting meetings. Describe specific behaviors or actions that your team . . .

Should *continue* what we already do not (for example, fill out all parts of the agenda to prepare for our meetings)

-

-

Should do *more* of (for example, clarify questions about agenda items in advance of the meeting when possible)

-

-

Should do *less* of (for example, jumping to the next agenda item before getting closure on the present topic)

-

-

Process Check #4

To be completed individually and then shared, followed by action planning

1. How would you rate
   ❑ Balance of participation?
   ❑ Sharing of opinions?
   ❑ Success in resolving conflicts?

   Low: 0%   50/50   High: 100%
   |·······································|
   |·······································|
   |·······································|

2. What resistance or reservations were expressed?
   ❑ Which did you explore directly?
   ❑ Which did you not really explore?

3. What reservations do you have about the approaches or methods your team is using?

4. How did you give suggestions on how to improve team processes?

5. How were your ideas received?
   ❑ Silence?   ❑ Compliance?
   ❑ Questions?   ❑ Attack?
   ❑ Directly, in words? ❑ Giving answers?

6. What facial and body language did you observe?

7. How would you rate the team's motivation to improve their approaches or methods?

8. How would you rate your own motivations to improve your team's approaches or methods?

9. What didn't you express to the team?

10. What would you do differently next time?

Process Check #5

To be completed individually then shared, followed by action planning

How clear were the team's goals and agenda for the meeting?

1	5	10
No apparent goals. Confusion about goals. No agenda.	Average goal clarity. Followed most agenda items.	Goals understood and accepted by all. All agenda items followed.

How focused was the team on the task(s) for the meeting?

1	5	10
Focused on topics not relevant to the task.	Most of the time spent on task.	Completely focused on the task.

How interested and concerned were team members?

1	5	10
Bored, uninterested.	Average level of interest.	Involved, concerned, interested.

How open were team members with one another? How freely were ideas and impressions expressed?

1	5	10
Defensiveness, caution, holding back.	Some restraint.	Openness in expression. Trust in others.

How effective was the decision-making process?

1	5	10
Teams could not reach decisions.	Decisions made by a few people.	Decisions made by team consensus or everyone's input.

How well did team members listen to one another?

1	5	10
Many interruptions, people ignored or talked over.	Some interruptions, people generally attentive to others.	No interruptions, frequent paraphrasing to ensure understanding.

How well was leadership expressed and leadership needs addressed?

1	5	10
Leadership not expressed; the team drifted.	Only some members exhibited effective leadership.	Leadership balanced among team members.

SYNERGY/COMMUNICATION EXERCISE 4
Constructive Feedback of Concerns

Workout Plan

When to use
When there is an apparent misunderstanding between members, when one member took action that caused a problem for another, or when communications are not working well.

Time
Varies, depending on the situation

Materials
None required, but writing out a statement can be useful preparation

Purpose/objectives

- To help team members deal with needs and concerns in real time, in a constructive way, directly with one another

- To allow members to improve their feedback capabilities and relationships

- To develop a habit of learning from events and leveraging what has worked, as well as improving those aspects that have not worked

Warm-up

Step back from emotions that frequently develop with problems or during times of communication breakdown. Mentally walk through the format to prepare your thinking and formulate your statement positively. Decide how best to interact with the other person—in person, on the phone, or on paper. Usually personal contacts are preferred because of the ability to work interactively through the concern to a conclusion that is satisfactory for both parties.

Aerobics

1. Follow the seven steps shown on the next page to formulate a well-planned statement.

2. Tell the other party you would like to offer feedback or would like an opportunity to work through something that has occurred. Ask if now is a good time to do that (if the answer is no, ask for a time that *will* work).

3. Make your statement.

4. Listen. Stay quiet and let the other person respond.

5. Be prepared to work through this to a common agreement, not to win.

Example

Sequence	Explanation
1. "When you . . ."	Starting with a "When you . . ." describes the behavior without judgment of inferences. The description is about specific behavior.
2. "I feel . . ."	Tell how the behavior affects you.
3. "The reason I'm telling you this . . ."	Say why you were affected that way. Describe the connection between the behavior and your feeling. Describe the consequence.
4. Pause	Allow the other person time to respond.
5. "I would like..."	Describe the change you want the other person to consider.
6. "Because..."	This is how it alleviates the problem.
7. "What do you think?"	Listen to the other person's response. Be prepared to discuss options. Remember, the receiver doesn't have to make changes.

Cooldown

Although many people dread giving "tough messages" or feedback about concerns to teammates, the openness of communication frequently makes for a clear, positive response that lays the groundwork for a stronger working relationship.

SYNERGY/COMMUNICATION EXERCISE 5
Stakeholder Commitment Check

Workout Plan

When to use
Use in planning strategies for gaining support and commitment of others who are key to the team's success. Stakeholders of the project can be defined as anyone who has the necessary resources, veto power, influence, ownership, or political clout to make or break project efforts, or anyone who will receive the product of your work or be involved in implementing it.

Time
One to two hours

Material
Stakeholder Commitment worksheet

Purpose/objectives
- To assess possible or probable existing attitudes key stakeholders may hold toward the project

- To ensure sufficient leadership to work through the natural obstacles of implementing and sustaining project outcomes

Warm-up

Set a ground rule for confidentiality of this discussion, because others who were not involved could possibly misunderstand the purpose and see this as criticism. The sensitivity of this work makes it more appropriate for a person-to-person conversation than for an email or fax communication.

Aerobics

1. List key stakeholder groups and/or individuals on the left side of the matrix.

2. Mark each with Xs and Os following the directions given to show present, perceived, and desired levels of commitment.

3. Analyze the matrix to determine where commitment gaps occur and which gaps must be filled to achieve project success.

4. Build strategies to gain the desired commitment with groups and/or individuals.

Cooldown

Actions will frequently include one-on-one work as well as team action.

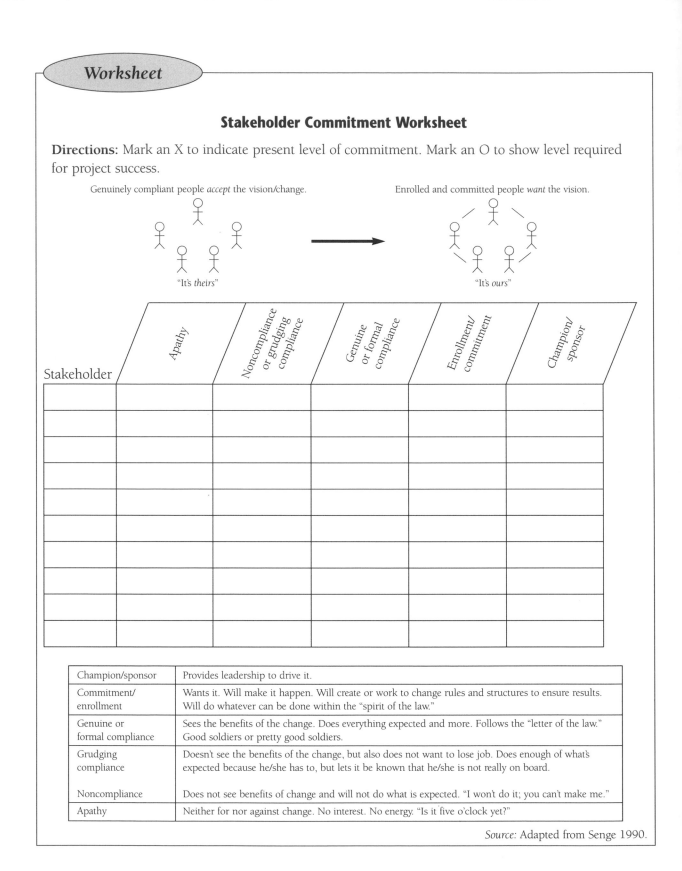

Worksheet

Stakeholder Commitment Worksheet

Directions: Mark an X to indicate present level of commitment. Mark an O to show level required for project success.

Genuinely compliant people *accept* the vision/change.

"It's *theirs*"

Enrolled and committed people *want* the vision.

"It's *ours*"

Stakeholder	Apathy	Noncompliance or grudging compliance	Genuine or formal compliance	Enrollment/ commitment	Champion/ sponsor

Champion/sponsor	Provides leadership to drive it.
Commitment/ enrollment	Wants it. Will make it happen. Will create or work to change rules and structures to ensure results. Will do whatever can be done within the "spirit of the law."
Genuine or formal compliance	Sees the benefits of the change. Does everything expected and more. Follows the "letter of the law." Good soldiers or pretty good soldiers.
Grudging compliance	Doesn't see the benefits of the change, but also does not want to lose job. Does enough of what's expected because he/she has to, but lets it be known that he/she is not really on board.
Noncompliance	Does not see benefits of change and will not do what is expected. "I won't do it; you can't make me."
Apathy	Neither for nor against change. No interest. No energy. "Is it five o'clock yet?"

Source: Adapted from Senge 1990.

SYNERGY/COMMUNICATION EXERCISE 6
"Must Do" Communications

Workout Plan

When to use
During the team start-up period when team members are trying to determine the ways they can move forward on their own as individuals and which ways they need to stay connected as a team.

Time
30 minutes

Materials
Masking tape and index cards if working face-to-face
Shared database if remote
Worksheet if working by phone or videoconference

Purpose/objectives
- To sort specifically between those areas that are "must do" communications between team members and those that are optional or "nice to do"

- To make clear the expectations for what is important enough to be communicated to other team members

Warm-up
Team members should generate a list of those items they each believe are "must do" and a list of those that are optional. If using index cards, put one idea on each card using large markers. Use a different color card for each category, *must do* and *optional*.

Aerobics

1. Team members read cards, list ideas one at a time, or post them on the wall or in the database for everyone to see.

2. For each item, the team reaches agreement on whether it is a "must do" or a "nice to do" communication.

3. Build a final list that goes to each team member.

Cooldown

Team members keep the list of "must do" and optional communications to refer to as they go about their individual work.

"Must Do" Communications Worksheet

Directions:

1. Each person brainstorms a list of team communications on 3 × 5 cards ("must do" or optional).
2. Place these cards either inside the box you've drawn on a flipchart or on the wall, or outside the box, as shown.
3. The team discusses, clarifies, and consolidates until a list is finalized of communications that "must" be sent to other team members.

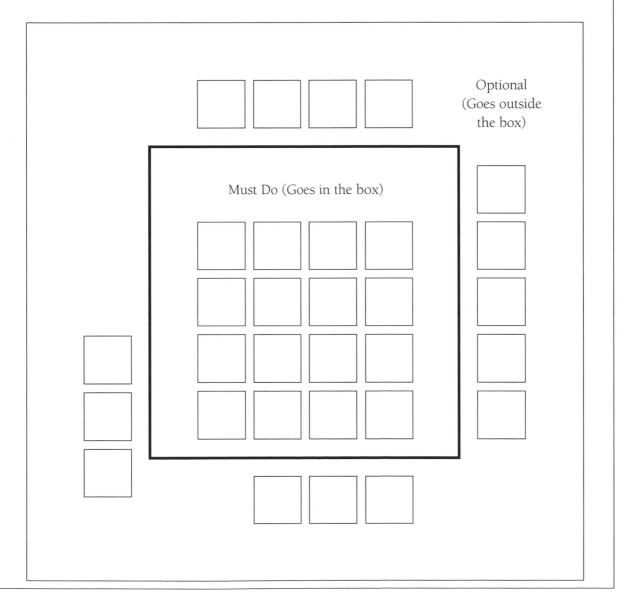

Optional
(Goes outside
the box)

Must Do (Goes in the box)

SYNERGY/COMMUNICATION EXERCISE 7
Communications Planning

Workout Plan

When to use
Periodically throughout the team project or work cycle, develop a plan for systematic communication that gets the right messages and information to the people who need them. This is a particularly good exercise to do at the end of "meaty" team meetings to ensure that the communications go right.

Time
30 to 45 minutes

Materials
Flip chart or wallboard if working face-to-face
Worksheet if working by phone or videoconference

Purpose/objectives
- To determine specific messages and information that are needed for specific audiences and in a certain time frame

- To make certain the messages that get to people are what is intended and that the communication happens clearly

Warm-up
Start with decisions or plans that have been put into place and need to be communicated within or beyond the team. Make a list or clarify exactly what needs to be communicated.

Aerobics

1. Use a separate planning sheet for each item that must be communicated. Write the message or content in the middle box (the box with the most room).

2. Underneath the message, determine activities/actions for how the message will be delivered. Use the four categories to group the activities. Answer these questions: What needs to be delivered verbally? To whom? By when?

3. Repeat this questioning process to generate activities for each of the four major channels. Don't forget to be creative. If you think of something effective that doesn't fit into the four categories, make up a new category!

4. Come to agreement on who will do what.

Cooldown

Each team member keeps the communication plan to work from. A good check at the beginning of the next meeting is to look at progress and make sure there has been followthrough on assignments.

Communication Plan

Message/Content—

Channel	Who	Activities	Timing
Verbal		•	
		•	
		•	
Written		•	
		•	
		•	
One-on-one		•	
		•	
		•	
		•	
		•	
Events (meetings, training, retreats, offsites, etc.)		•	
		•	
		•	
		•	

SYNERGY/COMMUNICATION EXERCISE 8
Energy Check

Workout Plan

When to use
At any time during the project.

Time
30 to 60 minutes

Materials
Energy Check worksheet

Purpose/objectives

- To acknowledge that fluctuations in energy are natural during a project's life

- To allow team members to help each other get unstuck in a low energy time

Warm-up
If team members are meeting in person, go around the group one at a time and ask members to describe their energy level using the descriptions on the Energy Check worksheet. If remote, ask team members to describe on the phone or write their description in the database, using the worksheet to guide their language.

Aerobics

1. Descriptions are compared to estimate the level of energy at the present time.

2. Plans are made for actions, encouragement, and support to help team members keep moving through the project toward desired results.

Cooldown

Each project team member may go through times of discouragement. Make sure there is sufficient time to work through people's concerns as you use this tool.

Energy Check Worksheet

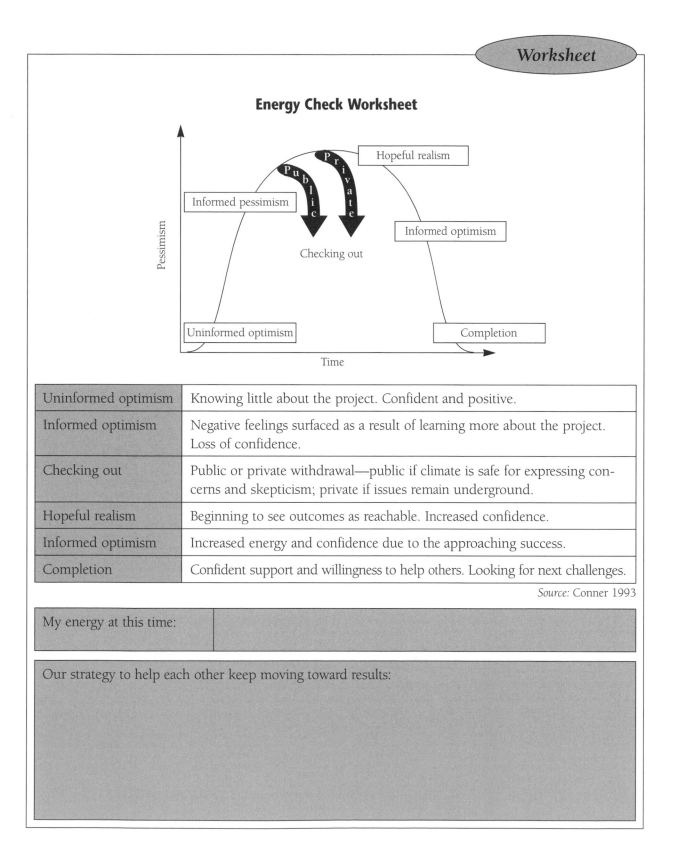

Uninformed optimism	Knowing little about the project. Confident and positive.
Informed optimism	Negative feelings surfaced as a result of learning more about the project. Loss of confidence.
Checking out	Public or private withdrawal—public if climate is safe for expressing concerns and skepticism; private if issues remain underground.
Hopeful realism	Beginning to see outcomes as reachable. Increased confidence.
Informed optimism	Increased energy and confidence due to the approaching success.
Completion	Confident support and willingness to help others. Looking for next challenges.

Source: Conner 1993

My energy at this time:	

Our strategy to help each other keep moving toward results:

SYNERGY/COMMUNICATION EXERCISE 9
Tapping Our Inner Resources

Workout Plan

When to use
Use this activity when the team is in the start-up stage and is preparing to take on its challenge. It is also useful when the team is facing a significant barrier and planning how to overcome that barrier. This activity is best performed in person and would be especially appropriate in a team start-up meeting.

Time
One hour

Materials
Inner Resources worksheet

Purpose/objectives

- To help team members get in touch with some of the intangible but significant strengths and resources they have developed from personal life experiences

- To help each team member know what the other members believe they can count on within themselves when things get difficult

- To bond team members to one another

Warm-up

Each team member takes the worksheet and spends time alone thinking about how to answer the questions, making notes to guide what will be shared with the team.

Aerobics

1. Team members share one at a time what they thought through and how they recorded their significant experiences, and the character and strengths that have developed as a result of those experiences.

2. After everyone has shared his or her thoughts, the team has an open discussion about the significance of the themes shared and how they relate to the project or the team's work.

Cooldown

To end the session, team members share one thing they learned or appreciated about the session that will be particularly helpful in reaching the goals of the team.

Inner Resources Worksheet

Think about some of the significant or profound events in your life. What were they? List three to five key events.

-
-
-
-
-

What are some of the positive values, beliefs, assumptions, qualities, and skills that you relied on and/or gained from these experiences?

-
-
-

How can you use these same values, beliefs, assumptions, qualities, and skills to help you contribute to the success of the project today?

-
-
-
-
-

Epilogue

As we said in the beginning, you are entering uncharted territory in working with your dispersed virtual team. Breaking new ground is exciting. It can also be treacherous. Hopefully, the ideas presented here will help you to avoid mistakes and help you build the synergy and creativity that teamwork can produce.

You will have the opportunity to bring together a high-powered, diverse group of people. You will be able to bring more talent to the work than if you all had to be co-located. Using the exercises we offer, your team will define your success. You can be clear about the direction of the team, its outputs, and how you will be measured.

To get there, you must build your own credo based on all members' values and competencies. Most people selected for your kind of team are extremely competent and accountable for results. You need clear values and agreements, not hierarchy, to guide your efforts.

You'll need to be clear about direction and focus, particularly up front, because you won't have the self-correcting mechanisms immediately at hand to change direction. You'll need to be clearer about vision, mission, and goals so that precious time and effort are not wasted. With your values and specific plans in place, you'll be positioned for success and accountable to one another and the whole.

Perhaps your most difficult challenge will be in the area of synergy and communication. Deliberate planning will be required to keep communication flowing. The technology is available to help with this. You must consciously learn to use it and agree as a group on how to use it.

Your virtual team is a reality for today and the future. What may seem exotic now will become commonplace. We excitedly wait to see how you take this new and challenging way to work and make it achieve breakthrough results for the twenty-first century.

We wish you the best of luck with your virtual team.

Meg and Jane

appendix a

Virtual Team Manager's Checklist

1. Are we clear about the outcome of the team's work? Are we a team that recommends things? Makes or does things? Runs things? (Katzenbach and Smith 1993)

2. Is everyone clear about the scope of our work?

3. Can every member state the vision, mission, and objectives for the team?

4. Does every member understand his or her accountability for output and the time frame?

5. Do we have the training and resources necessary to accomplish our mission?

6. Have we established a set of operating agreements based on our values and our organization's culture?

7. Does everyone know how to use the technologies and processes necessary to do the work?

8. Are our decisions and meeting minutes documented and distributed within 24 hours of the action?

9. Do we know something personal about how each team member prefers to work together?

10. Do we deal with incompetence and broken agreements in a timely and effective manner?

11. Do we deliberately build in some fun and celebration of milestones?

12. Do we regularly check in with customers and understand their current needs and requirements?

13. Do I communicate progress, changes, and problems up, down, and across the chain of command?

14. Do I check in with each member on a regular basis, formally and informally?

appendix b

Sample Plan for Start-Up Meeting of a Virtual Team

The first face-to-face meeting of a new team is of crucial importance. You have only one opportunity for this meeting, and it may be the only time when all team members are present. It is imperative that people get to know each other quickly, build trust and understanding, and become clear on the team's task and their roles in that task. We recommend the following 24-hour meeting at minimum for any team that will work together for a month or two.

Lunch

Plan for an informal lunch with some icebreaker activity, such as pictures and "minibios" of each member on the wall where people come in. This allows for different arrival times and informal introductions.

Sample afternoon meeting focus

Introductions. You will want to get people talking to each other comfortably as soon as possible. Go around the table and have each person share the following:

- Their experiences in working with a remote team—what went well and what could be improved; lessons learned

- Their experience with the project currently before them or other projects of a similar nature

- Why they believe they were chosen to be on this team

Record the data from each person on a flip chart to be copied and distributed after the meeting.

Present the Background of the Project—How It Came to Be, Any History of What Has Been Done, Why It Is Important. This may be done by a team sponsor, team leader, or team coordinator. It should delineate

- The output of the team

- How the output will be used

- The resources available

- Any parameters or restrictions

Focus the Heart of the Afternoon's Work on Direction Activities (see pages 28 to 53).

Evening. Adjourn the meeting for informal dinner and activities. This time should be spent talking about the day's activities, getting to know each other better, and having fun. Dinner could be somewhere that's comfortable and special to the area where the meeting is being held. For example, it could be a western setting, a typical southern place, on the waterfront, or whatever is indigenous to the area. Evening activities should be designed to allow for interaction—a barbeque, a baseball game rather than a play, or miniature golf with silly prizes rather than a concert.

Next morning

Have brunch available at the meeting site so that people can visit and talk informally about the previous day's activities.

Morning meeting focus

Focus the Heart of the Morning on Values, Agreements, and Communication (see pages 61 to 83 and pages 96 to 132).

Summarize agreements and assignments.

After the meeting

Record all information from the flip charts, including agreements and assignments. Mail or email materials to participants to be waiting when they arrive back at their remote sites.

appendix c

Example of Meeting Structure

1. *A clear statement of the purpose by the convener:* ("Why I think you are here," "Why I called this meeting," and so on).

2. *Clarification of objectives:* ("What will we have when we're done?" "How will we know that we've been successful?") Review desired outcomes of each agenda item.

3. Validation or modification of approach/process:

   - Ensuring a game plan of steps to accomplish the objectives (for example, problem statement, brainstorm, cause-and-effect diagram, storyboard, and so on, with time frames).

   - Agreement on ground rules: behaviors the group expects of its members during the session (for example, "keep it simple, "have fun," "be open and positive," "be willing to share your thoughts and feelings," and so on).

4. *Identification and clarification of roles:*

- Leader: who, what to do, what not to do, limits of authority.

- Scribe: who, how (flip chart or overhead notes), limits of participation.

- Timekeeper: who, what to do, what not to do.

- Facilitator: who, how works with leader, whether to focus on process only.

- Participants: responsibilities vis-á-vis other roles.

5. *Task work:* Work through the agreed-on agenda items.

- Use subgroups where appropriate to build effective people/skill combinations, to allow more effective use of time through parallel activities, and to allow individuals more air time.

- Be prepared to modify the procedure as you go to reflect the realities you encounter (vs. sticking rigidly to the structure).

6. *Process checks during the meeting:* Pause periodically during the process to check how it's working. That is, focus *both* on the effectiveness of your planned procedure and the satisfaction of members with everyone's behavior (norms).

- You can stop and say, "Let's pause a minute and check how we're doing, both in terms of our work output and working process." (You can free-flow it or go around the group.)

- You can use a structured process check (see pages 110 to 114).

7. *Bring the meeting to closure* by ensuring that all objectives have been met; review decisions made; ensure that responsibilities are clearly defined and time expectations are clear. This is also a good time to get a more thorough review of the whole process. You can ask people to identify "What are the things that helped this session be as effective as it was?" and "What are the things that kept us from being as effective as we could have been?" Use this information to develop what you would do differently next time.

   Tip: Revisit expectations to ensure that any topics left hanging have a follow-up plan.

8. *Make any necessary plans for follow-up,* including communication to meeting participants about implementation, decisions outside their control, and so on.

9. Set the next meeting's time and agenda.

   Source: Adapted from GE Plastics Commercial Education & Development

Bibliography

Armstrong, D. J., and P. Cole. Managing Distances and Differences in Geographically Distributed Work Groups. In *Diversity in Work Teams: Research Paradigms for a Changing Workplace,* edited by S. E. Jackson and M. N. Ruderman. Washington, D.C.: American Psychological Association, 1995.

Collins, J. C., and J. I. Porras. *Built to Last: Successful Habits of Visionary Companies.* New York: HarperBusiness, 1994.

Communications Company Gets Creative with "Virtual Staff." *Corporate Report* (1 June 1995).

Conner, D. R. *Managing at the Speed of Change.* New York: Villard Books (Random House), 1992.

Davidow, W. H., and M. S. Malone. *The Virtual Corporation: Structuring and Revitalizing the Corporation for the 21st Century.* New York: HarperBusiness, 1992.

Geber, B. Virtual Teams. *Training* (April 1995): 36–40.

Hartzler, M., and J. E. Henry. *Team Fitness: A How-To Manual for Building a Winning Work Team.* Milwaukee: ASQC Quality Press, 1994.

Katzenbach, J. R., and D. K. Smith. *The Wisdom of Teams: Creating the High-Performance Organization.* New York: HarperBusiness, 1993.

Larson, C. E., and F. M. J. LaFasto. *TeamWork: What Must Go Right/ What Can Go Wrong.* Newbury Park, Calif: Sage Publications, 1989.

Nagel, R. N. "The Virtual Corporation and Strategic Alliances." Presentation at PPI Midwest Conference, Iacocca Institute, Lehigh University, Bethlehem, Penn., 10 September 1994.

Senge, P. M. *The Fifth Discipline: The Art and Practice of the Learning Organization.* New York: Doubleday Currency, 1990.

Townsend, A. M., S. M. DeMarie, and A. R. Hendrickson. Are You Ready for Virtual Teams? *HRMagazine* (September 1996): 123–126.

Virtual Companies Leave the Office Behind. *Columbus Dispatch,* 21 April 1996.

Index

Comments and Areas for Improvement:
Tools for Virtual Teams: A Team Fitness Companion

ase give us your comments, feedback, and suggestions for making this book more useful. We believe in the importance of tinuous improvement and in meeting your needs. Your comments will help determine what improvements can be made in all Q Quality Press books.

ase share your opinion by circling the number below:

tings of the book	Needs Work		Satisfactory		Excellent	Comments
icture, flow, and logic	1	2	3	4	5	
ntent, ideas, and information	1	2	3	4	5	
yle, clarity, ease of reading	1	2	3	4	5	
ld my interest	1	2	3	4	5	
et my overall expectations	1	2	3	4	5	

read the book because:

he best part of the book was:

he least satisfactory part of the book was:

ther suggestions for improvement:

eneral comments:

Thank you for your feedback. If you do not have access to a fax machine, please mail this form to:
ASQ Quality Press, 611 East Wisconsin Avenue, P.O. Box 3005, Milwaukee, WI 53201-3005   Phone: 414-272-8575